STUCK IN THE STORM

Break free and grow beyond your past to a brighter future.

CASSIDY GLO NOVAK

SILVERSMITH
PRESS

Published by Silversmith Press – Houston, Texas
www.silversmithpress.com

Copyright © 2024 Cassidy Glo Novak

All rights reserved.

This book, or parts thereof, may not be reproduced in any form or by any means without written permission from the author, except for brief passages for purposes of reviews. For more information, contact the publisher at office@publishandgo.com.

The views and opinions expressed herein belong to the author and do not necessarily represent those of the publisher.

ISBN 978-1-961093-75-1 (Softcover Book)
ISBN 978-1-961093-76-8 (eBook)

This book is dedicated to the ones who have held me up in prayer *and* held my hand through the painful growing and healing process.

Other books by Cassidy Novak:

"Your mind is a garden. Your thoughts are the seeds. You can grow flowers, or you can grow weeds."

—WILLIAM WORDSWORTH

"Storms will always rage. Don't run from them. Some things in life can only be learned in a storm."

—PARKER S. HUNTINGTON

Contents

Foreword 9

Acknowledgments 13

Introduction 17

Chapter 1 – Weeds and Storms 21

Chapter 2 – Soil 27

Chapter 3 – Addictions 39

Chapter 4 – The Relationship with "Why" 47

Chapter 5 – It's a Heart Issue 59

Chapter 6 – When is Enough, Enough? 67

Chapter 7 – Forgiven *Not* Forgotten 77

Chapter 8 – I am Sorry 85

Chapter 9 – Worst. Day. Ever. 93

Chapter 10 – Choosing To Be Happy 101

Chapter 11 – Broken Vessel 113

Chapter 12 – Brain Game 125

Chapter 13 – Waving the White Flag 131

Appendix 142

Foreword

BY JOANNA K. HUNT
NYT BESTSELLING GHOSTWRITER,
BOOK STRATEGIST,
CEO OF SILVERSMITH PRESS

There are moments in life that are truly divine like the moment I first met Cassidy Novak. We were connected through a family member, another mom of triplets and little did I know how much like family we truly are. Cassidy and I learned we grew up in the same circles and share many friends in common, even though we live 1000 miles apart.

It didn't take long for me to see the fire and passion inside Cassidy to make a difference and leave a mark of healing and hope on this generation. And that's exactly what she's doing—touching hearts with her miraculous story all around the world.

Cassidy's first book, "I Can, I Have, I Will: Blooming Through Life's Greatest Tragedies" had a great impact on my life personally. Her story of overcoming and her press into faith through adversity are truly remarkable. Little did I know I would face an unexpected tragedy of my own shortly after Cassidy released that book and her word to "bloom" in the midst would resonate loudly in my spirit as an anchor of hope in the storm.

Now, in this book, *Stuck in the Storm* Cassidy has done it again, bringing a timely message packaged in grace, hope, faith, and determination.

* * *

Life can often feel like a series of storms, each one testing our resolve, patience, and resilience. *Stuck in the Storm* is a profound exploration of these challenges, offering not just a path of survival, but the tools and strategies needed to ground yourself and uproot every weed that would choke out the life of freedom Jesus paid for us.

Trust me when I say, very few people have the grit and tenacity that Cassidy has. She is truly equipped to share this poignant *now word* with all those who have *ears to hear*.

As you embark on this journey, consider how the lessons learned in this book might illuminate your own path and inspire you to keep pressing forward.

Stuck in the Storm is more than a book; it's a manual for resilience, a reminder that no matter how fierce the storm, we have the power through Christ to endure and emerge stronger on the other side.

Acknowledgments

Clif: Thank you for supporting my dreams. And making a way for them to happen! I am grateful for all you do each day and love you so much.

To my amazing kiddos: Your love and encouragement mean more than you'll ever know. You give me those hugs and affirming words just when I need them the most. Thank you for letting me take the needed time to write through the journey of life. I love you five so very much.

Mom and Dad: Thank you for your love and support as I continue to move forward and grow in ministry. Thank you for your help editing and feedback for parents navigating the tragedies in life. Love you so very much.

Sarah Ruth: You have been there through it all it seems. Thank you for your direct honesty in navigating the journey of writing this book and encouragement to face the struggles and "tough stuff" head-on. You are more than just family. Always have been, always will be.

Nicole: You've been my spiritual bulldog for years and faithful prayer warrior. Thank you for helping me re-focus when I was ready to throw in the towel. Thank you for prayers of protection and tough love when needed to face the music. Love you bookend.

Val: Thank you for the "bestie" therapy sessions on the phone and listening with your whole heart and not only hearing the pain, bur feeling it too. Thank you for encouraging me to keep going when I was weak and didn't think I could. Love you boo.

Lifies: Where would I be without you? It's truly a blessing when you walk through different seasons and find yourself back with those who prove that they are there to stay. I am the woman I am today because of going through the ups and downs with you. "Framily" forever.

Angela: You are one of the greatest cheerleaders in my life, and I want to thank you for your continual light you pour into my life, and my children's life. You weather the storms and truly care, and that is such a blessing to so many. Love you bosom friend.

Charlana: I am thankful for the lifeline you are in my life. Going back to my twenties, you have been there to mentor, encourage, and pray with me. I am so grateful for you.

Ms. R.: Thank you for always believing in me, and for your help editing the book. Your endless encouragement has helped me heal in many ways and I love you dearly.

Joanna: Thank you for helping me through another publishing journey, to go after it with my whole heart and stand strong in my beliefs. Thank you for being a dear friend and sister in Christ. Thankful for you.

Candice: Thank you for going to battle with me in prayer, and being there to encourage me with our photo shoots! Appreciate you and think you are an amazing artist in many ways!

To my readers: Thank you for believing in me and encouraging me to write book number two! I hope and pray it blesses you as you continue to grow and choose to bloom through anything you face!

Introduction

I was stuck. There I sat looking at the computer screen in complete shock at the prognosis the doctor had sent back with my test results. I had done the hard work, I had jumped all into a healthy lifestyle years ago, and diligently followed the regimen. And wait, I had been *miraculously* healed twenty years ago! What was going on? How could this be possible?! I was confused, angry, and honestly terrified of what the end game would be for not only myself, but my family as well. I had some crucial decisions to make at this crossroad in my life. And if I was completely honest, I was so exhausted that I didn't even *want* to try. After all, I had tried so many times before, and seemed to fail indefinitely. But how could I just *stay* where I was? What kind of a life would that be? We are only given one life, and I decided right then and there, I didn't want to waste another day being stuck.

We all face storms in our lives. Many of them take us off guard. And our human nature is to run away and not deal with what is at hand. But I learned something crucial to apply to whatever it is I am facing right now; how to navigate the storm.

Did you know when sailors come across a storm unexpectedly, they turn their ship and face it head-on—sailing *into* the storm? I've learned in order to heal and prosper in our lives; we need to do the same. What are the storms in life that we need to face? They can show up as heartbreak, trials, rejection, addiction, loss, sickness, betrayal, or even regret. *Storms* are anything that rains on our parade and threatens to sink our very existence. In a similar manner to charting the rough waters in our lives, we must learn to cultivate healthy heart soil. Healthy heart soil is a life that blooms with many things including happiness, confidence, and freedom. If we want healthy soil, we need to do the strenuous and dirty work of digging out those stubborn weeds. Those are usually self-soothing habits. Then we need to go after those deep roots- that can be our hidden secrets of shame. And also, we must remove the stones- those are often bitterness, unforgiveness and shame. Yes, the work will be gruesome at times, but the Lord showed me step by step it will be worthwhile to gain victory and breakthrough.

I wanted my life to bear fruit. What kind of fruit? Fruit such as peace, joy, healing and wholeness. Fruit that I could share with others too, to help them heal and grow. I had thought I had done a pretty great job of getting my soil healthy. But the Lord knew there was more I needed to work on. I started looking into my past, I adjusted my mindset in the present, and began planting seeds for a brighter future. In some areas I needed to repent of things I long ago buried. In other areas I needed to walk in complete obedience to what the Bible instructed me to do. The Bible provides a road map to our life, but we must follow the directions. The decision had been made, I did to not want to stay stuck any more.

There I was digging into the terrain of my heart with stubborn weeds and painful stones, and turning into hurricane winds and holding on with all I had. But wait, could it be? There was light on the horizon. I finally reached the point where the pain of me staying the same, was greater than my fear of change. And just like the sun breaking through the dark clouds, I was breaking through to freedom as well.

CHAPTER 1

Weeds and Storms

I carefully wiped the sweat from my brow with my muddy hands, trying to keep it from dripping into my eyes again. Earth was caked under my nails. New pink blisters emersed from my palms on top of old calluses. Dirt stuck in the creases of my arms, and my cheeks were bright red from all the shoveling that seemed to go on endlessly! Gardening is very rarely a pristine experience as presented in the movies.

I looked around, determined to not let these annoying pests win. How could it be that I already put down-not one-but *two* layers of landscape tarp, and new topsoil, and still weeds threatened to overtake the whole garden? And at the same time, I had been gingerly tending to my plants daily, watering and adding fertilizer, and there were barely a few buds!

There was only one plausible explanation to this. Even though I dug and dug, taking giant chunks of earth out of my garden at times, I must not have made it to the root of the weeds. By not removing the *entire* the root system, I unintentionally made those pesky weeds even stronger in their comeback.

Weeds—there are more than 8,000 species of them! Once you've had them in your garden, it's a daunting task to get rid of them. Weeds are much harder to control because they produce seeds and can spread by tubers, underground stems, and above-ground stems. Weeds are hearty and can survive in locations that are inhospitable to a more desirable plant species. Unlike most vegetables and fruits, weeds don't need the soil to be perfect to thrive.

We find similar conditions with the soil of our hearts. It *needs* tending. We have many deep-rooted weeds from past wounds, broken relationships, guilt, shame, and anger. We may even have stones in our heart soil buried so deep, we do not even realize they are there- but they *are* there. We must do the hard work to "work-out" our salvation and strive to live in health and wholeness. Just like healthy soil, a healthy heart produces fruit.

The Bible lists out fruit given to us from the Holy Spirit in Galatians 5: love, joy, peace, patience, kindness, goodness, gentleness, faithfulness, and self-control.

When we die to our SELF, we are making room to grow and become whole and redeemed through Christ. And that is when we produce the fruit of the spirit which is:

- Fruit to handle the hard situations in life correctly.
- Fruit to hold onto for nourishment through the drought seasons in our spiritual growth.
- Fruit to share with others who need help.
- Fruit to walk in love as Christ's ambassadors.
- Fruit to be light in the darkest of situations.

When cultivating a garden, there is more concern than just the annoyance of an unwanted weed. There are also species of *poisonous* weeds. You can lose your plants, and even some animals, if poisonous weeds take root. Like a trapper drawing in its prey with what appears to be a tasty morsel, the enemy tries to ensnare our hearts with poisons like unforgiveness and bitterness, that can not only ruin our lives, but those around us.

And then we have to contend with the unpredictable weather that can leave us in drought praying for rain, or horrendous storms that wash away our soil and damage our seeds and plants.

There are two parables in the Bible that come to mind. One being found in Matthew 7 explaining the importance of building our lives on a strong foundation, so they are not swept away in a storm. Another one is found in Mark 4 sharing a story about a farmer who plants the seeds on different types of soil and waits for the results at harvest time. Some seeds were not planted well and birds ate them up. Some seeds fell on rocky soil and were unable to take root. Some seed fell among thorns and weeds and were soon choked out. But the seed that was planted in good soil produced a good harvest. What is *our* harvest? Harvest is fruit such as peace, joy, contentment and healing in our lives. Once the seed of God's Word and promises are sown into our hearts, it is up to us to grow our faith.

Disintegration is another way the enemy works against us. When something is disintegrated it is made weaker by breaking it into smaller pieces until it is destroyed. It is the opposite of being whole, it is falling apart. The enemy does not want us healed and whole, so he attacks to try to break us down. But there is good news! We are in charge of our gardens, not the enemy. When we are walking out our journey to wholeness, it can *seem* undauntingly long, difficult, and messy at times, however it will also be freeing! The hard work is worth it in *every way*. Don't try to take shortcuts on your road to healing yourself from the inside out. You will only delay the progress and frustrate yourself. Anything of value comes from hard work and perseverance. There is a wise saying that applies well here, "Pain is temporary but quitting lasts forever."

Don't quit on YOU. If you want to have freedom from the bondages you are carrying, if you want to grow into the best version of yourself, if you want to succeed on your journey in life, then don't quit! It is the courage to continue that counts now more than ever before. Don't allow fear to handicap you as you start your healing journey.

Have you gotten to the place where the pain of staying the same, is greater than the pain of change? I think you have. I think you are ready. I think you will surprise yourself with the inner strength you will find on this journey. And if you are willing to look for it, you will find blessings along the way (or kisses from heaven as I like to call them!).

> "The only difference between success and failure is the ability to take action."
>
> —ALEXANDER GRAHAM BELL

CHAPTER 2

Soil

I believed the lie for many years that taking time for myself was selfish. "Mom guilt" is a *real* thing. Why is it that we feel guilty when we do something *by* ourselves or *for* ourselves? Why do we often have a critical eye peering at us for every move?

I have learned it is crucial to our well-being and those around us, to take time to refill our vessels. I was recently on a flight and reminded by the flight attendant as she went through the pre-flight instructions, "In case of an emergency, put your oxygen mask on first *before* helping others. Even if it doesn't appear to be filling with oxygen, it is working."

We have to breathe if we are going to help others breathe. What will we have to give others if we are running on empty ourselves? Whatever you have inside *will* come out. If you are rushing through a busy crowd with a cup full of hot coffee and bump into someone, that's what will spill out. Cold milk is not going to spill out of your cup. You spill what you have. If you keep stretching a rubber band eventually it's going to snap. In the same way, we snap when we are worn out, worn thin, and exhausted- physically, mentally, emotionally or spiritually.

Emotional exhaustion affects every area of your life. Have you ever been in a conversation with someone who was venting or unloading on you, and at the end you are the one feeling tired, weary, weighed down, or oppressed? That's because you are using up your emotional energy in those moments. You get to choose how and where you give your emotional energy. Your marriage, children, and family should be top priority and where you sow your time, affection, and love. Your job or ministry come after that. Yes, we are called to help others in their time of need, but it is crucial to minister to those the Lord has specifically placed in your inner circle first.

When you help others with a need it means you are pouring out, which also means you must refill your vessel after. How do you do that? By taking time alone to quiet your inner beings. This helps to steady your emotions and renew your mind. Taking time in the Word and in prayer fills and strengthens your soul and recharges you to pour into others yet again.

Often, taking a step back from certain situations helps you to gain a better perspective of the situation at hand. Jesus did this and is a great example to follow. He left the crowds *and* His disciples to spend time *alone* with His Heavenly Father—refreshing *and* refilling. What good are you if you are empty emotionally and stressed out? How does that bring peace, strength, or help to others?

I recently heard a sermon preached by Jordan Vale who said: "When you are whole- wholeness comes out. When you are fractured, brokenness comes out." *Our* soil needs to be healthy to plant in, and to carry seeds to help others plant as well.

What does healthy soil look like? It is rich, full of vitamins and nutrients, it has a healthy amount of moisture and is nourished by sunshine. Your heart's soil needs to be rich as well. You need to be healthy in all areas. You attain this through healthy habits, by getting needed rest, eating healthy, exercising, drinking plenty of water, and filling yourself with God's SON-light.

I really love the song, "Graves into Gardens" by Elevation. This song was written as a testimony to the power and authority of our God. We can confidently declare how faithful He is to each of us. God has the authority over *every* difficult situation in our lives, whether it be tragedy, loss, addiction, you name it, God can handle it *if* we invite him into our messes and struggles. As the song declares, the Lord brings *life* back to dried up dead bones! He is the *only* one who can turn our mourning into dancing and give us beauty in exchange for ashes. In fact, our God specializes in turning things around. But we must be willing to admit we have a problem, and hand it over to Him. None of us are exempt to needing the Savior.

Have you ever noticed it's so much easier to pick up a lazy, bad habit than to pick up a good one? I just hate that! And it seems at times, the negative consequences from our bad choices come about quicker than the healthy victories. I often joke that it feels like it takes forever to lose weight, and I gain five pounds just smelling French fries in the drive through line! Our habits didn't become unhealthy overnight, and we can't undo them overnight either. We must take the time to do the work to get our heart soil healthy.

When you start digging, you might encounter some rocks after getting past all the weeds. These are the scars deep down inside what you sometimes do not realize are there. You might find just a few pebbles; or you might find some boulders. Either way, you must get those out of the soil for your heart to have a healthy harvest. While digging, you might deal with some inconvenient storms in life. These bring excuses to stop digging and leave it be. But no more excuses, yes it's raining, so put on your rain gear and keep working. What is the "rain gear" to help us in these storms? I feel a good place to start is putting on our spiritual armor of God. We find a complete list in Ephesians 6:14-17, but I will focus on just a few. Let's start by putting on the *shoes of peace* like rain boots. These prepare us by being right with God and contended in trouble times. And we need to do everything within our power to remain peacemakers in all situations. That leads to blessings. Then, let's use our *shield of faith* like an umbrella. This protects us with knowing God will keep His promises. Faith in God protects us when we are tempted to doubt in those storms. And then let's put on the *helmet of salvation* like a rain bonnet. This helps keep our thoughts guarded remembering the truths of God's word.

Now that we are protected in the storm, it's time to work on digging up those stones. First, consider the tools you're using. It's crucial at this point to be completely honest with yourself and how you got to where you are. It's time to stop pointing the finger at others who have hurt you, the unfair situations you have faced, and the hardships you've endured. Yes, it's time to look at yourself in the mirror and deal with whatever ugly truths you may find. *You* might be the cause of those stones in your soil. Remember that quiet time I mentioned earlier? Well, it's time to get that journal out so you can start digging. Take a moment and quiet yourself. Then it's time to evaluate what's inside your heart. Take time to think about the following questions. Answer honestly according to what comes to mind when you think about these questions:

1. What happened to bring you to this moment in your life?
2. Who or what caused you this pain? Ask the Lord to bring to your remembrance individuals and *specific* situations where *pain* has occurred.
3. Choose one circumstance and go back to that moment in time. What happened? Write it out. Where were you? Who was there? How did you feel? Think of the specific details of the room or the setting around you. Look at the colors, listen for the sounds around you. Are there any smells that come to mind? What were you

wearing? Was there a certain food involved? Was it bright or dark? Inside or outside? Yes, *nitty gritty* details to let your brain *fully* process through what happened there in that memory of betrayal, fear, or pain.
4. Go there, then sit there for a moment once you have collected the details of that space in time. Imagine yourself in that moment again and call out to the Lord an ask Him to meet you in that space. Invite Him into your place of pain-your darkest hour.
5. Think of an object to represent your fear or pain during that time (I picture a red ball).
6. Acknowledge it. Don't ignore or suppress the pain you are feeling right here, right now. Face the pain, dig into it. Even if you're white knuckling it, hold on. This is what I call facing the storm!
7. Now pause. Breathe in deep. Hold it. Breathe out slowly and take the object of your pain and hand it over to God. In that moment, you are giving Him that person and that situation that has brought so much pain.
8. It is no longer yours to carry. In fact, *you were never designed to carry it.* You are not strong enough, and *that is okay.* Because this burden

you've carried for so long is now going into the Lord's hands. It's not your responsibility. Hand it over completely.
9. Next, it's time to release it for good. God gave us the tool of forgiveness to fully release our pain to Him. You see, forgiveness isn't about the other person, it's about setting *you* free. When you forgive, it doesn't mean what happened didn't matter. It means you are releasing it over to God. Say out loud, "I choose forgiveness. I choose to forgive (name) for (what they did)." Say it out loud over and over until you feel the release.

The key to this working is that *every time* you start to feel pain, anxiety, depression, or anger rise inside of you about certain people or specific situations, remind yourself (and continue to tell yourself) you have *already* given it to the Lord. Say that out loud again, "I forgive (name) for (what they did.) Don't pick up that offense and pain again. You can live in freedom!

Now, I'm going to give you the next step in healing a painful stone. I want you to find your *happy place.* This is a place you can go in your mind that brings comfort, peace, and joy. So where do you go that brings you one or all those feelings? Maybe for you it's the beautiful, majestic tall mountains where you can smell fresh clean air and pine trees. You can see a waterfall in the distance, and almost feel the mist on your face. Then you step into a cool babbling brook to soak your feet. You take in nature all around you and lose yourself in the moment. Choose a scripture verse that can meditate on such as Psalm 23, "He leads me beside still waters, and He restores my soul."

Or your happy place might be thinking of a lush meadow on top of rolling green hills with beautiful wildflowers all around you by the thousands. You smell their sweet scent in the warm breeze and the sun kisses your skin. You lay back in the soft grasses and majestic flowers watching the puffy white clouds go by. While honeybees and butterflies buzz as they float around you in pure bliss.

Or perhaps, like me, your happy place is on a beach somewhere where you can smell the salty air and dig your toes in the sand as you listen to the rhythmic waves crashing on the shore. Then you watch the glow of the sun setting over the beautiful ocean casting peach and rose colors all around in its full glory. Declare over your life John 8:36, "He whom the son sets free is free indeed!"

When triggered, remind yourself of the object of your pain that you gave to the Lord in that room and space in time. Then go immediately to your safe "happy place" in your mind, practice this till it becomes a second nature response. You are inviting peace into your inner being and calming your soul in this process.

Wherever it may be, find *your place* of peace and meditate on His Word when you feel anxiety, fear, or anger arise. Remember, "God has not given you a spirit of fear but of power, love, and a sound mind."

And the *really* amazing thing is, if you are willing to put in the effort and work, the results will be incredible! He turns our graves into gardens when we invite Him into our mess.

The more you dig up the stones in your life, the healthier your heart soil, and the healthier your garden. When your garden is healthy, you will bear much fruit that you can share with others. *This* is walking out a life of wholeness, sharing our harvest, and receiving God's grace for us every step of the way.

Jordan Vale said it perfectly, "Pursuing grace is not a life of perfection. Grace can't be managed or scheduled. Finding wholeness is not merely following disciplines and rules. It is found when our boundaries are shattered, and we learn by unlearning."

Do you feel exhausted just thinking about these steps to take? Well, an antidote to exhaustion is wholeheartedness. Have you tried half-heartedly or in your *own* strength for long enough yet? You can never fully move on and heal if you don't *deal* with the pain. It's time to hand it over to the Lord, releasing control, digging deep to unearth and throw away those stones.

CHAPTER 3

Addictions

There are many types of weeds that can grow our lives. One that is stubborn and has strong roots is found in the form of addictions. I think *every* person has struggled with an addiction at some point in their life whether it be with food, shopping, or pornography...the list goes on and on.

People who suffer from addictions deal with uncontrollable urges and compulsions to use dangerous substances or to engage in harmful activities despite knowing the negative consequences these may have on their lives, or how it affects those around them. Individuals who struggle with addiction physically or mentally are often unable to stop on their own. This is why we need God's power to set us free.

According to the Cleveland Clinic there are two main types of addictions: substance and behavioral.

1. <u>Substance addiction:</u> There nine *types* of substance addictions within this category (alcohol; caffeine; cannabis; hallucinogens; inhalants; opioids; sedatives, hypnotics, anxiolytics; stimulants; and tobacco). In 2019, it was recorded that over thirty-five million individuals worldwide struggle with substance addiction (or drug use disorders). Also, it was noted one in three households suffered from, was exposed to, or is otherwise impacted by addiction. I am sure these numbers have risen quite a bit in the last several years with all that has taken place globally.

2. <u>Behavioral addiction (or process addiction):</u> These are excessive behaviors identified as being addictive. They include gambling, eating, having sexual intercourse, using pornography, computers, video games, internet and digital media, physical exercise, and shopping. The International Journal of Environmental Research and Public Health reports that as many as forty-six percent of Americans suffer from at least one behavioral addiction. Imagine how those numbers have risen since the pandemic of Covid?

Who can become addicted? Anyone really, but there are many contributing factors. These include genetics, trauma, stress and depression, or anxiety disorders. Those who are genetically predisposed may find themselves more likely to develop an addiction if they suffer from chronic stress or abuse substances to cope with their problems or to create a numbing effect. According to an article in the International Journal of Preventive Medicine, a behavior can be considered addictive if it meets the following criteria:

- Salience: The person's life has become dominated by the behavior to an excessive extent.
- Euphoria: Does the person get a high, a buzz, or other feelings of intense pleasure from engaging in the behavior? (known as a dopamine hit)
- Tolerance: In order to get the same positive feelings, the person engages in the behavior more and more. They increase in destructive behavior patterns to try and get the same endorphins.
- Withdrawal: Ceasing the behavior abruptly can cause anxiety, irritation, frustration, depression, or distress. Isolation is very dangerous with addiction. We need accountability and support. We *need* community.

- **Conflict:** Regularly engaging in the behavior causes conflict with others or internal conflict. We react against others when we are at battle within ourselves.
- **Relapse:** The person returns to the behavior again and again, even though it is causing negative life consequences, such as poor performance at work or school, neglecting children or a spouse at home, or failing to meet social obligations.

Sadly, many individuals with behavioral addictions are more likely to have substance abuse problems as well as other psychiatric disorders like depression, generalized anxiety disorder, post-traumatic stress disorder, bipolar disorder, obsessive-compulsive disorder, and attention deficit hyperactivity disorder.

Bottom line, addiction is real and every year growing more rampant in our society. I took some time to list out important information about addictions because I think it's something we need to be aware of and knowledgeable about.

My husband and I have both dealt with different forms of addictions. Thankfully, we sought professional help and have gone through numerous years of support, therapies, and recovery groups to help us on our sobriety journeys.

I feel it is of utmost importance for each individual struggling with addiction to not in any way try to go it alone! It's not a weakness to realize you need help. If you have any hope of overcoming whatever your addiction(s) may be, *you must have accountability.*

What does accountability look like? Where do you start?

Step one: Admitting you have a struggle. No justifications.

If an individual is still justifying their destructive behavior, then they may not be ready for positive change. You cannot make a person change. Guilt trips, manipulation, withholding, rejection, anger, abuse, isolation, and/or threats never work. *You cannot be someone's Holy Spirit.* You cannot influence someone's conscience for a lasting change to happen. Sometimes, a person must hit rock bottom before they are at a place ready for change. And rock bottom looks different for everyone. When dealing with an addiction and working towards sobriety, the pain of staying the same must become greater than the pain of change.

I truly believe that for one to find freedom, he or she must find the root. And not only find the root but dig it up COMPLETELY.

It's time to get raw, real, and vulnerable. We want to grow and heal, right? Then it's time to start digging. Get your journal out and sit in a quiet place, *uninterrupted,* and answer these questions truthfully.

1. What are your addictions? Give a detailed list of *all* of them.
2. Where do you think your addiction(s) come from? Is it generational, from a form of abuse, etc.?
3. When did this negative behavior first start? Make yourself go there. Think long and hard about when it *first* began. Ask the Lord to bring to your remembrance. He will bring forth what you need to address.
4. What triggers your negative behavior? Is it a person, a place, an emotion, a certain action done to you *or* by you?
5. What is your false refuge? What you turn to, to soothe yourself when you are upset?
6. How do you "act out" when you are dealing with being **HALT**–Hungry-Angry-Lonely-Tired?

7. How do you respond when someone you trust lies to you or hurts you? Do you feel betrayed?
8. How do you respond when you have success or victories in certain areas? What do you do to celebrate?
9. How do you respond when you feel forgotten or looked over?
10. How do you respond when you are accused of something you did or didn't do?

Answering these questions honestly and thoroughly is a great place to start digging out those stubborn weeds of the soul, and learn to navigate high winds that come from storms in our lives. I pray you find revelational truths as you take an honest evaluation of your list. These lists are not inclusive. Often as we continue to grow in our lives, we have more revelations come to the surface in areas that need our immediate attention *before* moving on. Sometimes it's not just about our healing, but about us repenting as well. While writing this book I have had to add to my list and deal with more roots and some tornadoes myself. Let's keep working on it together!

CHAPTER 4

The Relationship with "Why"

I've said it before, and I'll say it again, life is unfair. You cannot control what happens to you, you can only control the way you choose to respond to it. Have you ever gone through a relationship or been in a situation where, if you could have seen what would happen, you would have avoided it all together? *If only* you had known? *If only* we could see the future, eh? *If only* we could know the outcomes of our decisions or the consequences of our choices. We cannot live with an *"if only"* mindset. We cannot change what we have done or what has happened to us. Regret entraps us, and quickly! Time keeps moving on, and we must do the same.

Growth opportunities find us in each season of life. Our priorities shift and change. It's important to remember that our purpose in life is not defined by one thing, a certain individual, or a moment in time.

God is continuously writing our stories, and with that comes much change and growth.

Opportunities for growth often come through our relationships. Some are easy, some seem impossible, some come and go, some give, and some take from our lives. It's time to learn how to navigate those relationships with a little more grace and wisdom. One good thing to learn is there are certain people who walk through life *offended*. Taking on offense can easily become a lifestyle if we're not careful. *No one is exempt from offense.*

"Negative Nellies" some like to call them, who are constantly upset with someone or about something. My husband Clif says, "If you're looking for something *bad* you will always be able to find it, no matter how *good* the situation may be." This goes for each of us. Being negative can *quickly* become a bad habit that is hard to shake.

I recently saw a quote online from Bryant McGill that said: "The feeling of being offended is a warning indicator that is showing you where to look within yourself for unresolved issues."

Focusing on our own wants and needs (being selfish) is also something many people struggle with. It's easy to think, "How does it make *me* feel?" But we need to get our eyes off ourselves and realize there are billions of other people in the world, and their feelings count too! Your life is not just about you.

If you are dealing with nonstop drama, headaches and heartaches in your life, and if you have problems within *many* of your relationships, whether it be at work, with family, or in your friendships, it's time to look at yourself and realize it can't *always* be the other person at fault. It might be *you*. Ouch! I know, right? I've been there. I have had to admit it to myself, more than once, it was me! I was the problem!

It's easy to get offended and to become upset. I struggle with it many days. But it is a *choice* to be miserable and unhappy with what life throws our way; and it's a *choice* to stay there wallowing in our misery. Happiness is also a *choice*. Being positive is a *choice*. Having a good attitude is a *choice*. And forgiveness is a *choice*.

This advice comes from an individual who has been diagnosed with clinical depression and anxiety. This comes from someone who is on medication and dealing with ongoing health issues and effects from a severe brain injury. I get it. I know it's hard. But we need to stop using past wounds, mistakes, heartbreaks, mental and emotional health issues as a crutch or excuse for bad behaviors. Everyone struggles with things. Even though each of our wounds, struggles, and strongholds look differently, that doesn't justify them or make them any worse than someone else's. If you're ready for some positive change and you're grabbing hold of this revelational truth, it should bring conviction and motivate you to healthier choices. But don't allow where you have been to swallow you up in shame. Shame and guilt are not the same thing.

Verywellmind (Dotdash media, Inc.) states:

- **Guilt** is a feeling you get when you did something wrong, or perceived you did something wrong.
- **Shame** is a feeling that your whole self is wrong, and it may not be related to a specific behavior or event. They go on to explain that over time intense feelings of shame can take hold of a person's self-image and create low self-esteem.

There is new research on the role of biology in the development of shame-based low self-esteem which can come from low serotonin levels in the brain. I believe that was a large contributing factor for me. I did a SPECT brain scan years ago and found out my brain was producing only three percent serotonin.

THE RELATIONSHIP WITH "WHY"

This resulted not only from my life-threatening brain injury, but they were able to gauge the damaged tissue going back to my childhood when I suffered a concussion. I give these details to offer some insight into the lasting effects head injuries can have on a person. I had the typical concussions from falling off my bike, one of my horses, and in cheer leading. Often, after taking the appropriate amount of time to heal, people return to normal life and activities. But what isn't taken into account is there can be, and often are, lasting effects on our brain from these injuries. This affects our mental and emotional health as well as the way we cope and respond to certain situations.

If you are struggling with certain things such as anger, insomnia, OCD, depression, or anxiety, *and* you have had a head injury of concussion in your past, make sure you share that helpful information with your health care provider so you can get the correct diagnosis and treatment you need.

Shame also can come from *any* form of abuse, which I had to overcome as well. We will dive into further details of overcoming abuse a little later.

Now back to dealing with those individuals in our lives that are very hard to have relationships with.

It's time to learn about *healthy boundaries*. It's time to realize having healthy boundaries is not a bad thing *or* a selfish thing. Having healthy boundaries is a crucial part of *staying* healthy. Being around negative/critical people is draining and you can find yourself quickly falling into similar unhealthy patterns. So, you must define what *your* boundaries are and *keep* them in check!

How does one define boundaries, you ask? First, let's look at what a boundary is:

- Setting personal boundaries is when you place limits and rules within a relationship.
- These "rules" create a *healthy distance* between individuals.
- It's being able to comfortably say "no", and to accept when someone else says "no" to you.
- Healthy boundaries within a relationship are when both parties are able to safely communicate their wants and needs.
- It is honoring and respecting your own needs and the needs of others.
- Healthy boundaries mean sticking to your personal values and beliefs, and not compromising. It is respecting other's values, beliefs, and opinions, even if they are *different* from your own.

So how do you figure out what your boundaries are? You need to take time to tune into your emotions and what your heart is telling you. How do you feel in certain environments around certain individuals? Do you feel drained, heightened stress or anxiety? When you tune into your emotions you better understand what is working for you and what isn't. Tune into what thoughts you are having around certain individuals as well. How are you feeling about yourself or towards others after interactions with a specific person or group? How do you react and respond when you have been hurt and are angry?

I have also found it can be helpful to ask others to share what some of their boundaries are and what has worked for them in similar environments or relationships.

It's crucial you know what *your* values are. If you don't clearly know what is important to you and why, you won't be able to protect it.

If you have a bag of apples and one spoils in the middle, every apple it touches will rot if you don't remove it. The good apples around it do not make the rotten apple healthy again. The Bible tells us similarly bad company corrupts good character.

Haven't you noticed how easy it is to get caught up in gossip or criticizing other people? My mom always said if someone is talking about others in front of you or to you, you'd better believe they are talking about you behind your back. The Bible warns of the devastating effects of gossip. It goes on to say that if you participate by sitting there, not leaving or stopping the conversation, you are just as guilty as the one gossiping.

There is life and death in the power of the tongue. What are you speaking? What are you saying about the individuals in your life who drive you up the wall and you can't seem to win with them no matter how hard you try? Who are you venting to about the individuals who HAVE hurt you, or new drama they brought, or frustrations that come your way? You will be held responsible for *every* word you say, and for influencing someone else's opinion towards them.

Those hard to deal with individuals are in *your* life for a reason. Yes, that's a hard pill to swallow; but they are. Usually, it's because *you* have some growing to do yourself. Perhaps there is something in your character that needs to be worked out and perfected through the help of the Holy Spirit. Unfortunately, similar situations will continue to come your way until you have grown and learned the correct way to respond, and then to be able to move on in a healthy manner.

But what if we have continually shown love, grace, and forgiveness to no avail and they still are impossible to deal with? They are there in *your* life for a reason.

What if they refuse to forgive or work on healing the relationship? They are still there in *your* life for a reason.

But why? Because there is something for *you* in this relationship. It may just be an opportunity for growth, or it could be for you to plant a seed in their rocky soil and water it with some grace and love.

As we learn to walk in grace, we are learning to grow in the process. However, it is crucial for you to guard your heart and not overextend yourself in unhealthy ways trying to win their favor or approval. Keep those healthy boundaries.

The Bible uses the analogy of placing pearls before swine. Let me clarify. I am *not* telling you to go to unhealthy measures to try and prove a point or make amends. Trust the Lord and His timing for direction on this relationship. Be led by Him in what you should do, ask for wisdom and strength to know *how* to move forward, and choose patience to wait for His perfect timing.

When you have God's approval, that's all that matters. God knows the heart of *every* individual involved and the *complete* truth in all situations, and that's what you need to cling to. From my experience, the truth will always come out. The light can and will expose the darkness.

Let's be honest, some relationships are downright toxic and abusive. These need to be kept at arm's length and handled with much prayer, and sometimes with fasting as well. This is why it's important to determine what your boundaries are and consistently implement them.

Within these types of relationships, it is not wise to engage in emails or texting as a form of communication. Nor is it wise to communicate alone with the individual. Do not allow them to guilt or manipulate you into a conversation you do not feel safe having. Do not let them pressure you into doing *anything* you are not comfortable doing and you do not have peace about. Take time before you decide to be around these individuals. Especially if there is a negative track record with that person. Does this individual manipulate the conversations they are a part of? Do they disrespect your time? Do they twist your words around and use what you have said as ammunition against you? Do they talk about others while they are with you? Do they criticize and accuse you of things you didn't do? Do they use you or take advantage of your kindness and hospitality? Do they take and never give back? Remember the importance of guarding your energy and time. Toxic individuals are *energy suckers*. They are often time suckers as well. Remember, you will never get your time back.

Sometimes, you don't have a choice but to be around individuals like this. At this point it is crucial you keep them at a safe length and keep it **SSS–simple-short-sweet.**

- Treat them respectfully.
- Don't make a scene.
- Don't give into their baiting.
- Don't give into their dramatics.
- Don't participate in negative conversations.
- Don't engage in talking critically about others, *especially* other family members.
- Be respectful, be kind, but *be firm* in your brevity.

If you are in an unhealthy relationship that is causing grief in your life, it's time to take a realistic look at the depth of what is going on. Your life may be better off with this relationship taking on a *less inclusive* role in your life; not only for *your* health and well-being, but for your family's sake as well.

You can forgive someone without letting them back into your inner circle. The Lord must do the work on changing offended hearts. Remember, there is nothing *you* can personally do to fix a toxic relationship. Be wise with your time. Be wise with what you invest. Why, God, why? Because you *are* capable of handling this with the Lord's help and growing through this opportunity. You're here for a reason, so why not bloom in this process? I wrote an entire book on this very concept. Say out loud: *I Can, I Have, and I Will!* The choice is yours.

CHAPTER 5

It's a Heart Issue

It's a sad reality when no matter what, some individuals refuse to change destructive patterns or forgive others. That usually comes from a place deep within them, *a heart issue*. That is why it is crucial that you get these deep roots and stones out of *your own heart*, so you don't stay "stuck" in the storm weighed down with offense. That will lead to a life full of regrets.

Sometimes, our greatest heart issues come from not forgiving ourselves. We *all* make mistakes. We all have fallen short. We all have hurt others. We all have sinned. We all have lied. We all have disobeyed. We all have done things we regret. That is why it is so important to accept God's gifts for us. God is waiting with His hand outstretched to help us navigate the crazy world we live in. But we must invite Him into our hearts to be our Lord and Savior. We all need rescuing! What is amazing is He gives us unmerited favor, mercy and grace. And when we confess our sins, He is faithful and just to forgive our sins and cleanses us from all unrighteousness. He forgives us completely and keeps no record of our wrongs.

This gift is free, but we must open our hearts to receive it. I have found this is not a one- and-done gift exchange. The next time you mess up, you're going to have to unwrap that gift no matter how undeserving you feel. If we don't accept His love, grace, mercy, and forgiveness for ourselves, then we won't have any of those gifts to extend to others.

What if **you** are the one dealing with having a hardened heart feeling numb to most everything and everyone? I would say work on softening your conscience then this will help soften your heart as well. Have you noticed the printing at the beginning of mature audience shows or movies? It states, "Viewer discretion advised." This means that even adults should make a *conscious* decision whether to watch it—and be **very** careful about letting children see it. Our eyes and ears are the gateways to our souls, and what we watch and listen to *greatly* affects our hearts. This in turn affects the way we see, respond, and handle situations in our own lives. Matthew 6:22-24(NIV) says,

"The eye is the lamp of the body. You draw light into your body through your eyes, and light shines out to the world through your eyes. So, if your eye is well and shows you what is true, then your whole body will be filled with light. But if your eye is clouded or evil, then your body will be filled with evil and dark clouds. And the darkness that takes over the body of a child of God who has gone astray—that is the deepest, darkest darkness there is."

Most people agree that we live in a horrific world full of sexualism, violence, idolatry— the list goes on and on. I believe it all goes back to a heart issue. We have become desensitized as a society. Did you know that modesty is a heart issue? It is so much more than the way we dress. How do we present ourselves? Do we seek out attention and status with others?

When we become desensitized, we lack empathy for others. When we are jaded in *our* thoughts, we lack respect for others. When we are self-focused on *our* wants and needs, we lack compassion for others. The result is that sometimes we build walls out of fear, but it is a false sense of protection. There's a *difference* between *guarding* our hearts and *closing-off* our hearts. Those who have had difficulties in relationships and past wounds must learn how to navigate the difference. It's okay, even necessary, to protect yourself and those you love. It is not okay or healthy to burn bridges and shun people.

The more our hearts are hardened, the less we hear that "still small voice" of guidance from the Holy Spirit. You can read about it in the story of Elijah found in 1 Kings 19:11-13.

If you are feeling numb to life right now, ask yourself what have you been filling your time with? What have you been feeding your soul? What have you been watching? What have you been listening to? Who have you been spending your time with? This helps you figure out your patterns and paths you regularly take. That is your starting point.

Then, you need to make yourself choose a different path to lead you to a softer heart and outlook on life. How do you do that? Make a list, take inventory of what you do, who you do it with, and why. It's going to take some time and effort to get out of unhealthy patterns of living and thinking. It's not effortless to weather a new storm, but healing your heart and the way you respond to others and relate to the world around you will be worth it. Remember, what you put in does come out. It's just a matter of how and when, *and* who it will affect. Matthew 15 confirms that what comes out of your mouth is a result of what is in your heart.

It's easy to stay on the same paths we have always taken. Sticking with the *same* responses, the *same* coping mechanism and the *same* ways we self soothe. It is fighting your flesh to go a different way, but you can blaze a new trail with what you fill your mind with. The shows you watch, the music you listen to, and the people and environments you surround yourself with. We need peace in our lives and that comes from keeping our minds steadfast on Him (Isaiah 26:3). Meditate on His word and precepts. Write them on the tablet of your heart and renew your mind daily spending time with Him. This will soften your heart. And it will bring clarity to your mind.

If you are in a relationship with someone who has a walled-off heart, pray for those walls to come down. Pray the Lord softens and takes down their defenses, so they are approachable. Seek their forgiveness for anything you may have said or done to add to this wall of defense. *Many* walls come from wounds. When we get hurt, we don't want to go through that pain again so we try to protect ourselves by shutting others out. But the Lord can lead us through that pain and help us learn to guard our hearts in healthy ways without closing off from giving or receiving love.

I think it's important to point out that we know a person's character by the fruit we see in their life. Actions speak louder than words. When things get hard, when you experience difficulties in your life, look who will set those personal issues and offenses aside to be there for you. Someone who *truly loves* you will be there for you or your family in the time of need.

Parents and mentors, it's important to teach kids not only about self-esteem, but about respect, compassion, and empathy for others as well. It is crucial to point out to them that in order to maintain healthy relationships, you must focus on the wants, feelings, and needs of the other person, *not just your own*. We each have to tap into empathy with others, and if empathy is not a strong suit, it can be learned, practiced, and mastered. Growth in this area does not happen overnight. But with the help of the Holy Spirit, our hearts can soften, and we can become more empathetic towards others. Each of us have been a victim to someone's lack of compassion and empathy towards us. Let's strive to not inflict that pain onto others. Initiate goodness and kindness in this world. Do your part and be the light and love of Christ!

Remember, the words we speak reveal the *true* nature of our heart. Thankfully, the words we speak can also *transform* our heart and the hearts of others too. Speak life!

"For out of the abundance of the heart the mouth speaks. For by your words, you will be justified, and by your words you will be condemned"

(MATTHEW 12:34B, ESV).

CHAPTER 6

When is Enough, Enough?

If you or someone you know is struggling with abuse, know this: it is never okay. No matter the situation, no matter the history, no matter the explanation, bottom line abuse is never your fault, and it is never justified. My encouragement to forgive others is not a "green card" to place yourself in a harmful situation. You can forgive someone and not be in a relationship with them.

So, when is enough, enough? If you, or someone you know and love is in danger from a relationship, *any* form of abuse should never be tolerated—physical, emotional mental, spiritual, psychological, or financial. Taking care of yourself, means you need to consider *their past* behaviors so you can make better choices for *your future.*

Toxic behavioral traits come in many different forms and often build up over time in a relationship.

How do you know if someone is abusing you or someone you care about? Ask the following questions:
1. Is there manipulation in any form?
2. Are you being coerced to think you are crazy or something hasn't happened that has, and deal with distorted realities or justifications?
3. Are you being physically, sexually, or verbally harmed?
4. Are you not being respected and listened to when you say "no" to someone or something?
5. Are you being held captive and isolated from others?
6. Are you controlled and not allowed to make your own decisions? Is there power and imbalance in your relationship?
7. Are your personal problems or needs trivialized, criticized, or minimized?
8. Are you being humiliated purposefully or dealing with uncontrollable jealousy?
9. Are you dealing with someone who is possessive, has unpredictable outbursts of anger, or negative behavioral patterns?
10. Do you feel like you have to "walk on eggshells" and carefully consider what you do or say to not trigger the other person?

11. Are you blamed and punished for things out of your control, or things you didn't do?
12. Are you living in a constant state of confusion within your relationship(s), that sometimes it's good, and sometimes it's intolerable?

In my book *I Can I Have I Will* I share about my healing journey from sexual abuse in my childhood and adolescent years. I had suppressed my abuse so much that it did not resurface until after an extensive brain injury. Forms of suppression and acting out are common when you've endured something tragic in your life that is too hard to bear. Your brain goes into "survival mode" and compartmentalizes what happened. However, it is important to reach down deep to do the hard and messy work of processing, feeling, forgiving, and healing, so you can find freedom and restoration from *all forms* of abuse in your life. If you don't deal with what has happened to you, it can lead to a lifetime of pain and regrets. If you don't deal with what has happened to you, it will not only handicap your relationships, but your relationship with yourself and Jesus Christ. If you don't deal with what happened, it can lead to many forms of illness including mental and emotional problems. Unresolved conflict and unhealed wounds can lead to anxiety and depression. Depression can take over many aspects of our lives and it needs to be taken seriously. I will go deeper into sexual abuse later. I have been there; I have contemplated ending my life. I know how hard it is to choose happiness when you can barely get up and breathe in and out. I have been there in the lowest of valleys where I felt everyone would be better off without me. Yes, in the past I have considered taking my life more than once. *How could a person whose life was spared and miraculously healed even consider that?!* Because depression and anxiety are *real* and *heavy* to carry. Shame and guilt often feel like a load too great to bear. At those low points in life, I was believing *lies* from the enemy that everyone would be better off without me. I believed my life was a mess, and that I was too much of a mess to receive true healing. I kept hurting others and felt like a failure and a disappointment. But the *truth* is you and I are here right now, for a reason. We each have purpose. When we are a threat to the enemy, he attacks much harder. His retaliations are real, but our strength in Christ dominates it all! Fight back! Put on your armor found in Ephesians 6:10-18 NIV:

> "Finally, be strong in the Lord and in his mighty power. Put on the full armor of God, so that you can take your stand against the devil's schemes. For our struggle is not against

flesh and blood, but against the rulers, against the authorities, against the powers of this dark world and against the spiritual forces of evil in the heavenly realms. Therefore, put on the full armor of God, so that when the day of evil comes, you may be able to stand your ground, and after you have done everything, to stand. Stand firm then, with the belt of truth buckled around your waist, with the breastplate of righteousness in place, and with your feet fitted with the readiness that comes from the gospel of peace. In addition to all this, take up the shield of faith, with which you can extinguish all the flaming arrows of the evil one. Take the helmet of salvation and the sword of the Spirit, which is the word of God. And pray in the Spirit on all occasions with all kinds of prayers and requests. With this in mind, be alert and always keep on praying for all the Lord's people."

Your life is important. You are needed here—even if your life has been full of tragedies. Even if you have been abused and abandoned. Even if it *feels* like you have no one who cares. Even if you've made terrible mistakes. Even if you've failed time and time again. You are never too far from grace. There is hope available for you and God will take the pain of the past and use it to produce the purpose for tomorrow! You are loved, you matter, you are needed here right now.

Over 703,000 people die from suicide every year. In fact, in 2021 suicide was the tenth leading cause of death in the United States. It is the fourth leading cause of death among fifteen- to twenty-nine-year-olds. There are around one hundred and thirty suicides every day, that's one every forty seconds in America alone!

This is alarming! There are so many people who don't understand how valuable they are! What is happening in our culture that is pushing people to this breaking point? Is it a rise in pharmaceuticals? Is it a rise in mental illness? Is it a rise in fear and comparison due to social media in our faces constantly? Is it a rise in anxiety because our brains are over stimulated and never have time to rest? Is it because we are not dealing with and healing from forms of abuse in our lives? Scholars seeking explanations for this troubling trend have pointed largely to a decline in mental health due to increase in social media exposure.

Whatever the reason, something must change to stop this horrific trend. John 10:10 tells us "The thief comes to steal, kill, and destroy," but Jesus came to

WHEN IS ENOUGH, ENOUGH?

give us life abundantly! If you want to see change, *you need to start being the change.* Each of us has the power to begin a ripple effect to help many. You can help implement change by becoming healthy yourself. The work is hard, but the reward is so worth it!

If you are struggling with thoughts of ending your life, please reach out for help. Call 988. That is the Suicide and Crisis Lifeline, available 24 hours a day via phone, messaging, or chat. It's important to connect with someone who can help you navigate through your feelings and thoughts. Do not isolate. Do not attempt to go it alone. You need reliable help, and that's okay! I'm going to say it again, you need community! Your life is valuable and important! You are loved and needed! Connect with someone you trust and let them know *you are not okay.* That is not being selfish. Take some time for yourself, you matter. Take a moment to ask God to reveal Himself to you. He is there, and He promises to never leave or forsake you.

> "It is the Lord who goes before you;
> He will be with you. He will not fail you or abandon you. Do not fear or be dismayed"
> **(DEUTERONOMY 31:6 AMP).**

I started this chapter about abuse, which causes many to feel hopeless. Remember beautiful one, your life is important, and you matter. Your mess can become your greatest message. And in the words of Dr. Suess "To the world you may just be one person, but to one person, you may be the world."

If you or someone you know is in an unhealthy or abusive relationship, it is *crucial* to seek immediate help. You must act now because the next time could be the *last* time. Don't live with any regrets. Don't be silenced anymore; find your voice. You deserve freedom. You deserve to heal. You deserve to be loved and appreciated for who you are. You have value, you have worth. You are here for a reason, and you are important. Don't let anyone else lie to you and convince you otherwise. Your value does not diminish from another person's inability to see your worth.

If you are being abused on any level God does not require you to stay in an abusive relationship–right now, enough is enough. Yes, the Lord can redeem and work on anyone, *but you are not their savior.* They must be willing to admit that they are doing is wrong and be willing to change. You cannot be the Holy Spirit to them, and you cannot make them change. If this has been continually happening, stop believing the lies when they tell you that they won't do it again. See it for what it is—manipulation. If a person is truly sorry, they get the help they need, and they don't do it again. They won't tell you they will change—they just change.

If you are not sure if you're dealing with abuse, speak to a trusted adult or professional and explain in *detail* the situation at hand—everything you are going through, the good times and the bad. Oftentimes. abusers will "love bomb" lavishing you with love after a harsh event. It's a dysfunctional cycle. The highs are as much abuse and manipulation as the lows. It is important that you be completely honest about the nitty gritty details. Tell you story. Don't leave anything out, no matter how embarrassed or ashamed you feel. Victims of abuse often justify or excuse what is happening or has happened in the past because they are groomed to believe they deserved it. I want you to give yourself permission to trust your gut, you know in your heart if something is not right. Remember, forgiving that person does not mean you have to continue offering someone trust who is untrustworthy, or to continue in relationship with them. Moving on to a *safer* life is not something you should feel guilty or ashamed about.

Think of the others you would tell to seek safety and get the much needed and deserved help. You deserve that same safety and help! Love yourself right here where you are in your mess and say enough is enough! You are valuable and you are not defined by what has happened to you. You have the ability to change your story starting right now. Take that first step–even if you are afraid.

When you take a stand and distance yourself from abuse and toxicity, you are letting the individual know their behavior is unacceptable and it needs to stop. In a way, taking care of yourself is showing genuine care and concern that you want them to get the help that they need to heal and grow. Their behavior is not tolerable for you or for them.

But no matter what, it's time to get the help you need. Your life and future depend on it. And others who you may not even be aware of are depending on you too. Others are watching your next move. They might find their boldness and bravery to take a step after they see you stand up for yourself and find your freedom. It's time–enough is enough!

CHAPTER 7

Forgiven *Not* Forgotten

Over my life, I've been known to be someone who forgives quickly and easily. I can recall many events of being taken advantage of throughout my lifetime from doing so. Primarily, this came from my own insecurities and not knowing what true forgiveness is. Many problems ensued from my knee-jerk response to give people access to my *inner* circle after I forgave them. I didn't realize that relationships and forgiveness are not mutually exclusive. It was not wise on my part. Yes, it is *crucial* we forgive others. However, it is just as important that we draw clear boundaries until the person has changed and has demonstrated a track record of change. Be careful who you allow in your *inner* circle. When someone shows you who they truly are–believe it the first time! Keep those healthy boundaries in place.

In that same way, you shouldn't go to deep levels with everyone. That's what healthy boundaries are all about. This is an area where I have had many growing pains. I desire to have close relationships, but the truth is, not everyone is trustworthy, and not everyone has your best interest at heart. There are people that will never support you because it's *you; and* there are people who will always support you because it's *you*. Ask the Lord for wisdom to discern the levels and depths to go in each relationship. We need to ask for discernment regarding who is *for* us and *against* us.

Have you heard that there are two types of people in the world? Givers and takers. It's true. And it's up to us to have healthy boundaries to not overextend ourselves in giving of our time, energy, talents and resources. People will take and take as much as you are willing to give. Make sure those who are in your inner circle are balanced and willing to both give and receive from you. Guard those relationships. This is where you need to invest of yourself and your time.

I recently saw a post on social media about *true* repentance and learning to trust others again. There were some very valid points that impacted me, one being that you do not have to offer trust to someone who is untrustworthy. In my previous book, I shared that when we feel we *can't* trust the other person, it is encouraging to know we *can* trust God. There are numerous verses in the Bible that reassure us God cannot lie. Two verses I encourage you to press into when having trouble trusting are Hebrews 6:18 and Titus 1:2.

Trust must be regained through a change in actions over time. That change is also known as repentance. You need to see actions that mark a changed heart, a sign of true repentance. Here are some examples of what *true* repentance looks like:

1. The person will take personal responsibility for the wrongs they have done without excusing or blaming someone or something else—no justification.
2. The person will take the initiative in healing the relationship. It won't be you doing all the talking and pursuing to reconcile or reconnect.
3. The person's behavior will match their words—actions speak louder than words. And not just temporarily. There will be consistency over time.
4. The person's level of defensiveness will be significantly reduced, and the person will be approachable.
5. The person will have a desire to hear your perspective—not interrupting but truly listening.

6. The person will have remorse for how they impacted you and the wounds you are dealing with.
7. The person will make a commitment to do whatever it takes to truly change, then follow through with it consistently.
8. The person will have a long-term plan that supports and implements the positive changes that must be made.
9. The person will acknowledge, own up, and apologize when "slip ups" occur and old behavior surfaces. These slips should become less frequent over time.

When it comes to relationships and reconciliation, it's important to take time to P.A.U.S.E. before making any important decisions, especially where emotions or wounds are involved:

P- pray
A- ask
U- utilize
S- seek
E- endure

- PRAY—against the voice of the enemy, others, or yourself. God is not the author of confusion or fear.

- ASK – the Lord to help you hear His voice clearly above all others. Ask for wisdom, direction, and the answers you need.
- UTILIZE – the tools He has given you – the Bible, prayer, and Godly counsel.
- SEEK – the hidden truths found in reading His word and spending time getting to know Him better.
- ENDURE – no matter what comes your way, choose to stand strong and carry on.

It is pivotal to be led by the Spirit in *all* you do. The health and well-being of your life, and the lives of others, might depend on it so don't ignore that "still small voice" giving you warnings.

Recognize there is a difference between emotions and promptings. We should never be led by our emotions. Emotions are a byproduct of our thoughts which change on a regular basis. Our minds can play many tricks on us as we work through emotional events.

I can remember one time when I was pregnant with the triplets. I was hormonal and completely exhausted, and I lost it on my husband for eating my left-over steak. Yes, I was sobbing on the floor in the kitchen in what I felt was the worst moment ever! I literally started laughing when I looked at myself in the mirror after! Raise your hand if you too have had a knee-jerk reaction after feeling hurt about something. Let's just say I should have cooled off first. I have put my foot in my mouth on more than one occasion and made the situation much worse. *Rash decisions and actions are rarely right.* That's why we must P.A.U.S.E. and seek the Lord on *every* decision we make and before we speak out on a touchy issue. Reacting in the heat of the moment is almost always wrong. Allow yourself to calm down, or even take a day or two before addressing the issue. Wait for peace before you proceed. Wait for those emotions to calm down!

When you live a life yielded to the Holy Spirit, you will hear Him more clearly. When you follow the Holy Spirit, your thoughts will align with His thoughts, and your ways will agree with His ways.

Recognize that there's a difference between conviction and condemnation.

- **Conviction** is an awareness, prompting us to change. It's the acknowledgement we have done something wrong, that leads us to repentance. It comes from God and is necessary for growth and healing. It offers a high definition of clarity and it is helpful and brings hope.

- **Condemnation** is guilt and shame over something, with no space for growth and change. It focuses on consequences and punishment for your actions. It is lies from the enemy, leaving one feeling hopeless (Romans 8:1). Condemnation is also about punishment, or a sentencing. Christ came to redeem us from the sentence of death and offer us eternal life through Him! He brings the opposite of condemnation.

When we respond to or make a decision based off guilt and shame, we are not waiting and listening to the Lord. He will lead us in the next step *if* we seek Him and wait on Him to give us the prompting to move ahead.

Long ago, my mom told me an analogy that I still refer to sometimes. When you are dancing closely with a person, you allow them into your intimate space. You can feel yourself being led by them and going across the dance floor of life. But if this individual *continually* stomps on your feet and leaves you wounded, you must learn to hold them at arm's length, guarding and protecting yourself.

No, I do not apply the saying "forgiven and forgotten" anymore. Nor do I tell others to just forgive and forget like nothing ever happened. Yes, we forgive every single time, but personally I think it's wise to *remember* what happened. With this remembrance, we learn to implement healthy boundaries moving forward. Time to decide on who is in your inner circle.

CHAPTER 8

I am Sorry

I am sorry. These three simple words can greatly impact a person's life. How could such a simple and short phrase be so difficult for some individuals, that they never gather the courage or choose obedience to share them? I believe it comes from a root of pride.

Pride is known as one of the deadliest of sins. Pride alienates us from God. C.S. Lewis said, "[Pride] is the complete anti-God state of mind. It is 'The Great Sin' that leads to all other sins because pride is the exaltation of *Self* above all authority, even God's authority."

Pride can rear its ugly head in our lives in many ways. It can be boasting of self-importance and achievements. It can come out in our justifications of our wrong attitudes or actions that have brought about negative consequences and pain for others. In an essence, pride comes from a place of drawing attention to self.

We often judge someone else when they hurt or offend us and see it as a serious sin, but when it comes to us offending others, we justify ourselves saying we didn't mean any harm, or that we were just joking.

When we judge others, it does not define who they are; it defines who we are. Pride is also shown in impatience and lack of empathy for others. The scriptures say that pride deceives the mind and hardens the heart. It brings about contention and stirs up strife in relationships.

Proverbs 16:18 says, "Pride goes before destruction, a haughty spirit before a fall." It is described as a disgrace in Proverbs 11. Pride is often thinking less of others because of insecurity. When you are *looking down* on others, you can't truly know God; for our gaze must *be looking up* to keep focused on Him. We find in Colossians 3 the importance of setting our minds on things above, not on earthly things. I think that earthly things can be a distraction and hindrance in our personal growth. Why? Because it shifts our focus.

The Bible calls us to humility, which is the opposite of pride. Humility is an extension of love. We find an excellent definition of what true love is in

1 Corinthians 13:4-5, "Love is patient, love is kind. It does not envy, it does not boast, it is not proud. It does not dishonor others, it is not self-seeking, it is not easily angered, it keeps mo record of wrongs."

To *truly* love is to die to oneself or in other words to let go of selfish ambition. Pride is wrapped up in the pursuit of self. What *I* want, what *I* feel, and what *I* need. When you have pride, you cannot see your *own* faults *clearly*. You must be willing to own up to *your* sins and wrong doing. You need to acknowledge and repent as soon as you recognize you have hurt others too.

Your health physically, mentally, emotionally, and spiritually is affected by the well-being of your soul. You can't separate the two, it's not possible. As I write this book, the Holy Spirit has been doing a major detox in my heart, bringing up things that I didn't even realize I needed to take ownership of and apologize for—things from over twenty years ago! Things I thought nothing of and believed I had moved past; things that were *stones and roots* in my heart that I needed to dig up. These roots were deeply intertwined into the person I had become. I had created this person from my justification of what had happened to me, and how I protected myself. Or, so

I thought. Little did I know I had created a couple decades worth of strings rooted to pride that tainted my view and scarred my heart.

I had to take an honest look in the mirror and it was not pretty. In fact, the deep-rooted pride was downright repulsive to me. I wept. How could I have naively gone so many years choosing ignorance in vain, unwilling to look at the pain and destruction I had caused others? I had broken biblical covenants. I did not realize it at the time, but that didn't change the fact I had done it, or the consequences that followed. I came to the shocking realization I had possibly been the cause of someone else harboring unforgiveness or dealing with a root of bitterness for what I had done to them. Oh, I "ugly" cried. I asked the Holy Spirit to reveal to me and show me *clearly* those I had hurt at any point of my life. I decided right then and there, I would do whatever was within my power to apologize to those I had wronged. This is referenced in Matthew 5:23-24. I spent a few weeks sitting with my thoughts and wrestling with my convictions.

After I spent some time processing with the Holy Spirit and in prayer, I went to my husband and shared what the Lord had revealed to me. He prayed with me and supported me moving forward to make restitution with some of the individuals the Lord showed me I had wronged.

It is so important to do the hard work, and to do soul searching.

So often, we find ourselves guarding against a place of getting hurt again. We don't want to open ourselves up to feel the pain again! Especially, when we have walked through some form of abuse, or affliction from a toxic relationship. But that false sense of security can cloud our judgment, preventing us from seeing where *we* erred in our *own* lives, and how we have hurt others as well. We need to own up to what we have done wrong. We need to apologize if we have wounded someone, even if unintentionally.

Take a moment to sit in a quiet place with the Heavenly Father. Ask the Holy Spirit to show you *clearly* those you have wounded. Then repent *completely*, leaving no stone unturned or root undug. Be led by the Spirit on what your next steps are. *Wait* for His guidance and perfect timing. Remember from the last chapter to PAUSE- Pray, Ask, Utilize, Seek, Endure.

Do not step out in emotion. That could prove more detrimental than good. Remember, you are seeking to bring healing and freedom, *not* to ease your conscience. It is also important to be on the same page with your spouse before moving forward to contact a member of the family or maybe a past relationship. Be a unified front on any decisions to move forward in making amends. No blessing can come when going against your spouse or hiding inappropriate contacts with a member of the opposite sex. Step forward in honor to *everyone*. *Truly* question what your motive is. Guard your heart. Don't let your mind go to the "what ifs." No good can come from digging up the past within a former relationship unless you are *clearly* called to do so in repentance.

When you apologize to someone else, you might not get a welcomed response or any response at all. You might indeed step on a hornet's nest. So when you pray ask for wisdom with how to respond to any backlash, or if you should respond at all. Not all feelings are worth pursuing or trying to understand, some are just lies that we shouldn't feed into. Remember, you are not apologizing to gain man's approval. You are apologizing out of obedience to the Lord and to heal wounds all around.

What if you have been hurt and never received an overdue apology? It is important for you to forgive them completely regardless. Not for them, but for yourself. You cannot live a life in freedom or to the fullest when you harbor unforgiveness towards anyone, no matter how great or small the offense.

"Once you own a mistake, it no longer owns you."

CHAPTER 9

Worst. Day. Ever.

Have you ever had one of those days when everything that can go wrong does? Every little annoying thing that might happen has indeed happened. You find yourself staring in the mirror at a disheveled lunatic with steam coming from your ears, ready to explode. Then one of those precious kids you love so much drops a bowl full of cereal and milk all over the floor. Never mind that you had just told them not to get it because it was too close to dinner. Warning! Warning! Mom's about to lose it! It's time for what I call a "mommy time-out."

And yes, I literally put myself in time-out. I have learned the hard way that if I don't walk away from stressful situations, I will say things in the heat of the moment I later regret. Oh, I have many sad regrets in this area. Often our biggest gifts are also our biggest problem areas— mine being my mouth!

As a mom of five, with a set of triplets in the mix (in fact they were our firsts), *and* who homeschools, let me tell you I have fallen short many times! I love my kiddos so much, but in that mix of five, I don't have *one* laid back *or* quiet kiddo. They are full of energy and emotions every single day. It's like staring in the mirror, pay back times five of what I put my parents through! But on those long days when I can barely walk myself up the stairs to start the bedtime routine, I remind myself to take the time for *each* one of them. They are my sunny delights; in fact, they bring joy wherever they go! I want to make sure to focus on their gifts and reiterate to them what a blessing they are to me and everyone they encounter. I do this to help combat the chaos or consequences they may have faced during the day. I feel it's crucial we apologize to our kids when I am wrong and respond from my emotions. I have this down pat. And though I may lack in other areas and I'm not "mom of the year," I know one thing for sure–*I apologize to them every single time I get it wrong.*

Something else I try to implement often is what I call the *grace card*. This is a pass, so to speak, given even though a punishment is deserved. We *all* need grace. And on some of our worst days, when we can't seem to get anything right, that is when we need it the most. To the best of my ability, I want to show my kids Christ's love, and that means apologizing *and* giving grace.

Did you know research has found it takes five compliments to cover one insult given? The same ratio is suggested to combat negative thoughts. I have been learning that my reactions usually come from my *inner* turmoil. When I need an attitude adjustment, it is almost always because I am upset with *myself* about something. Then I struggle with taking it out criticizing everyone around me with unrealistic expectations of "perfection" that can never be met! And where does that inner turmoil come from? *My own issues with control!* When I don't meet the standard, when I don't meet a goal, when I mess up and someone is upset with me, the fear that I am a failure quickly follows. This is an unhealthy cycle that can be damaging, especially to those closest to us. We tend to take things out on those we love the most because we know they will be there no matter what. But they still deserve our love and respect even on our worst of days.

So, what causes so much stress and turmoil? It is often self-generated, being in a hurry, rushing through the "to do" list, and running to all the things that fill up the calendar. Rushing the kids to get ready and out the door. Rushing to finish an email to get to the next meeting. Rushing to finish the dinner and dishes. Rushing to the next ballet rehearsal or soccer practice. Rushing to the next gate for a flight. Rushing to get through bedtime to get to the laundry. The lists go on and on. It's a crazy, frazzled frenzy that is *not a* healthy place to exist. Why? Well for many reasons; it affects our relationships, our sleep, our mental and emotional health which then leads to problems with our physical health.

The Bible has given us a road map to follow on the journey of life. Did you know the fourth commandment is to remember the Sabbath and keep it Holy? God commands us to *rest.* As a society, we have allowed the Sabbath, the day of rest, to lose its importance. Sabbath is about us letting go of control and letting our Creator restore us. I recently heard someone say, "We were meant to work *from* a place of rest, not work *for* a place of rest." To come into a place of receiving the rest we need, we must have the correct heart and attitude towards taking a Sabbath. We must be attentive to the presence of God. Only then can our vessels be refilled.

Burnout is a *real* thing affecting many people today. HelpGuide.org lists burnout as a state of emotional, physical, and mental exhaustion caused by excessive and prolonged stress levels. It occurs when you feel overwhelmed, emotionally drained, and unable to meet constant demands. Remember how I mentioned it affects your *physical* health? Burnout takes on many symptoms including headaches, stomach/intestinal issues, fatigue, frequent illness, being more susceptible to colds and flu, and it changes your appetite and sleep patterns. If constant stress has you feeling helpless and exhausted, you may be on the road to burnout. It doesn't happen overnight, it's a gradual process. You may be thinking "I'm so stressed, this must be me!" But there is a difference between burnout and stress.

Stress involves *too much*; too many pressures that demands too much of you physically and mentally. It is characterized by *over*-engagement. Emotions tend to be over reactive, and often one struggles with urgency and hyperactivity. Stress leads to lack of energy and anxiety disorders. The primary damage for stress is *physical*.

Burnout, on the other hand, is about *not enough*. It's characterized by *dis*engagement. It leaves one feeling empty and mentally exhausted, with no motivation and lack of caring. It leads to detachment and depression. The primary damage is *emotional*. Burnout is not caused solely by stressful work or too many responsibilities. Other factors contribute such as one's lifestyle and personality traits.

As a society, we rarely turn off our minds to rest. Remember, *every* aspect of our body, mind, and spirit *needs* rest. What we do in our downtime, as well as how we view the world, plays a big of a role in causing overwhelming stress. Just like work and relationships and home demands do. HelpGuide.org also states that burnout recovery requires the "Three R" Approach:

Recognize–watch for warning signs of burnout.
Reverse–undo the damage by seeking support and managing stress in healthy ways.
Resilience–build your resilience to stress by taking care of your physical and emotional health; and I will add in your spiritual health!

We need to *reach out* when we are *stressed out* and *burned out*. We need each other. Community is crucial to a healthy lifestyle.

Did you know that social contact and interaction is an antidote to stress? Talking face-to- face with a good listener is one of the fastest ways to calm your nervous system and relieve stress. Another proven helping tool is giving to others. Being helpful to others brings pleasure and significantly reduces stress. Getting our minds off *ourselves* and onto others helps every time! Remember we have a limited self-view; we only see what we see. But God sees the big picture, the end from the beginning and He connects us with others who can help change us for the better. He brings people in and out of our lives in different seasons, and He does it all for our good.

When you are in a hurry you miss out on the present. There is meaning in every step of your journey, including the moments of today. Find the balance in your life. Think for a moment about what fills your love tank and rejuvenates your soul. It's time to find time for *more* of these things! If you are stressed out or burned out, you are empty and have nothing left to give to others, it's time to refill your vessel. Spend time with the Lord in prayer, with worship and in His Word. Fill yourself up to overflow!

Romans 15:13 says, "Now may God, the inspiration and fountain of hope, fill you to overflowing with uncontrollable joy and perfect peace as you trust in Him."

Go ahead and grab that pen and paper and jot down at least five things that bring you joy, peace, and comfort. You are looking for things that make you happy and bring excitement when you think of them. For me, some of my vessel filling comes from running, reading, salt-soak hot baths, girl's nights out and the like. Your list might look completely different than mine, and that is just fine. We are all uniquely different. It's time for you to explore what makes you tick—not what ticks you off! Write down what feeds your soul. What adds value to your life? And then, make sure you do it!

Psalm 16:8-9 NIV says, "I keep my eyes always on the Lord. With Him at my right hand, I will not be shaken. Therefore, my heart is glad and my tongue rejoices; my body will also rest secure."

CHAPTER 10

Choosing To Be Happy

Happiness has a broad range of definitions and explanations from different individuals all over the world. One thing I've experienced in my own life is that happiness is indeed a choice, and the choice is solely ours. For some, that may be hard to believe, but let's take a deeper look. Verywell mind defines it as an emotional state characterized by feelings of joy, satisfaction, contentment, and fulfillment. They go on to explain that psychologists and other social scientists typically use the term "subjective well-being" when they refer to the emotional state of happiness. Subjective well-being is just as it sounds, it focuses on an *individual's* overall personal feelings about their life in the present.

I see two tripping stones in this philosophy. One, being that it is *self*-focused—how do "I" feel, etc. Secondly, it focuses only on the *present* part of life. More about that in a minute.

Aristotle suggested that happiness is *the* one human desire, and all human desires exist as a way to obtain happiness. In fact, he believed that there were four levels of happiness:

1. Happiness from immediate gratification.
2. Happiness from comparison and achievement.
3. Happiness from making positive contributions.
4. Happiness from achieving fulfillment.

Let's dissect Aristotle (Ha! Not something I thought I'd ever find myself saying!). First point, "Happiness from immediate gratification." Though this may be true at times, it will seldom be *lasting* happiness. Let's use the example of sin. I came up with an acronym to describe sin:

S- Self
I- Interest
N- Navigation

Did you know sin in Hebrew is an archery term that means "missing the mark"? Sin often feels good in the moment and convinces us it is a *sure* ticket to happiness, because it will bring *instant* gratification. But sin over-promises and under-delivers every single time. You can never know the degree of the consequences that will come from that "*self*-gratification." You also won't know the extent of the effects it will have on those around you. The *instant* happiness you seek will *not last* when it is focused on making your*self* happy for you, and *you* alone.

Psalm 119:36 ESV says, "Incline my heart to your testimonies, and not to selfish gain!"

Second point, comparison is a thief of joy every single time! The Bible warns against comparison, it refers to it as *coveting*. What does it mean to covet? To covet is to yearn to possess or have something that belongs to another; to desire, wish, want, or crave inordinately exceeding reasonable limits, culpably, or without due regard for the rights of others. The Bible warns us to banish all desires for whatever does *not* belong to us.

Luke 12:15 ESV, "Take care, and be on your guard against all covetousness, for one's life does not consist in the abundance of his possessions." God further breaks it down with specific examples in His Word:

Exodus 20:17 ESV says, "You shall not covet your neighbor's house, you shall not covet your neighbor's wife, or his male servant, or his female servant, or his ox, or his donkey, or anything that is your neighbor's."

Desiring, or coveting, what someone else has will never lead to happiness. On the contrary, it will lead to a miserable life, feeling like we're missing out. It also keeps us from appreciating all the blessings in our own life.

Aristotle then refers to achievement coming after comparison. Though it may be good to have some healthy competition at times in our lives, I don't think "going after" the same success or possessions as someone else will ever lead to happiness. Instead, you will find that you've never *fully* arrived and will continue to compare and be disappointed with your shortcomings. Your life is your own, stop trying to live someone else's. Stop trying to "keep up with the Joneses." Their lawn needs to be mowed, weeded, and watered, too.

Third point, I can get on board with this one! Making positive contributions or helping others will always lead to happiness.

Acts 20:35 NIV says, "In everything I did, I showed you that by this kind of hard work we must help the weak, remembering the words the Lord Jesus himself said: 'It is more blessed to give than to receive.'"

When we are struggling with depression or we are not happy, if we get our minds *off* ourselves and onto others it leads to happiness each and every time.

Fourth point, happiness is achieved from fulfillment. I partially agree with this one and here is why. When we set a goal for ourselves and seek to achieve something, it feels fantastic when we accomplish it! But what about the times we fail? What about the times we fall short, and the achievement wasn't what we hoped for or expected? Does that mean we can't be happy? *Au contraire!* Our happiness *cannot* be based on our accomplishments because we will fall short every time. We are never done growing or achieving things in our life. We cannot wait for happiness to come from fulfillment, because we will never be fully satisfied or fulfilled in this present life.

Proverbs 27:20 NIV says, "Death and destruction are never satisfied, and neither are human eyes." This brings me back to diving deeper into the topic of happiness being self-focused and in the present. No one and nothing else can be responsible for your happiness. It's an unrealistic expectation that will leave every party involved frustrated and hurt in some form.

I feel blessed to have had a fairy tale whirlwind romance with my husband, from the way we met, got engaged and then walked down the aisle one year to the day after being paired together in a wedding.

Y'all, I was a small-town girl that moved to the suburbs of Chicago and left behind everything I had ever known. I was in culture shock and quickly fell into depression missing my family and friends. I relied on my husband Clif, to be my everything–and things went south quickly. In my heart I had wrongly placed him above God. Clif, of course could not meet my unrealistic expectations–no one could! I was let down again and again because lasting happiness cannot come from someone or something else.

Our fairy tale quickly came crashing down to a reality of addiction, infidelity, and rage as past wounds reared their ugly heads. I had to hand my husband and marriage over to the Lord as we stepped into a time of separation. Our triplet daughters were only two years old and I knew I had to go on living my life regardless of what happened with my marriage. Let me tell you, that was the harshest reality to face of all. At this crossroad, I realized my true and lasting happiness could only come from my Creator, Yahweh. He gave us our emotions and personalities for a reason, and while they can sometimes be our biggest struggle, they are still a blessing. If you call upon the Holy Spirit to help mature you, then you can grow to be the best version of yourself as you go through the toughest seasons in life. "Growing-through" will bring about much joy, *if* you hold tight and refuse to give up through the growing pains.

If you lost everyone important to you and everything of value, you could still choose to go on living your life in happiness. Would it be hard? Oh, my goodness, yes! But is it possible? Yes! Why? Because true, lasting happiness comes from finding your identity in the One who created you to be here right now, not only living your life, but knowing that He desires that you thrive and enjoy your life.

John 10:10b NLV says: "My purpose is to give them a rich and satisfying life."

Other translations say He (Jesus) came so we may live life more abundantly.

I recently experienced another bout of depression that lasted for a couple of months. It was frustrating and exhausting. I hate the weighed down feeling of no energy, minimal motivation, feeling tired no matter how much sleep you have, and the crabby moods that follow. It's crazy how quickly a bad mood and negativity can come on. I found myself miserable and upset with myself that I was in a funk I couldn't shake off. As a result, I was snapping at everyone close to me. But you know what? I refused to stay stuck. I made myself get up and get out. I took walks,

I made myself go for runs to clear my head and lift my mood. I made myself do devotions even though I felt "blah," and then write in my journal what I was thinking, feeling and what I was grateful for. I made myself get out of the house and sit in the sun while homeschooling my kids. I also made sure to reach out to my accountability partners and share about my current struggles. I was feeling angry with myself for these struggles and I quickly fell into old self-soothing patterns with food and anxiety. I needed to nip it in the bud before things accelerated. And I kept doing this day in and day out, week after week, until I was able to crawl out of it. I share this to be vulnerable and transparent that I don't have it all together and I still have struggles! I am a work in process (we all are), but *we must be willing* to do the work.

> I recently read in *The Mind Journal* a wonderful lesson on what we choose:
> Marriage is hard. Divorce is hard.
> Choose your hard.
>
> Obesity is hard. Fit it hard.
> Choose your hard.
>
> Being in debt is hard. Being financially disciplined is hard.
> Choose your hard.

Communication is hard. Not communicating is hard.

Choose your hard.

Life will never be easy. It will always be hard. But we can choose our hard.

Choose wisely.

So, you may be wondering how am I to choose to be happy, if it's solely up to *me*, but I'm not to be *self*-focused? Sounds complicated, but it's pretty simple if we break it down. *Every* day, in *every* situation, it's ultimately your choice how you will respond, and what you will do with it. How do you turn lemons into lemonade? By *choosing* to change your attitude.

You *choose* to focus on the good in your life. There is always good to be found somewhere. You can *choose* to help others even when you are going through something hard yourself. You can *choose* to get up and get out into the fresh air and sunshine. You can *choose* to stop negative talk about your situation and *choose* to speak life into those around you. You can *choose* to focus on the Lord and go to Him with a heart of gratitude because He is who He says He is! You can *choose* to praise and thank the Lord for all the things He has done in your life and the blessings He has brought your way. You can *choose* to notice kisses from heaven every single day. You can *choose* to shift your focus to the positive and not dwell on the negative. You can *choose* to live in a healthy mindset and in healthy patterns physically, mentally, emotionally, and spiritually. You can *choose* to forgive those who have hurt you and stop a root of bitterness from growing. You can *choose* to dwell on the fact that the sun will shine again even when going through the darkest of storms. You can *choose* to see the best in others and yourself even through shortcomings and pain. You can *choose* to embrace that You are part of a bigger picture and that *right here* and *right now* is not your *final* destination. You can *choose* to face hard situations with a mindset that it is a great opportunity for personal growth. You can *choose* to love the unlovable with God's help. You have the option to *choose* to turn the crummiest of days into days of joy. You can *choose* to dance in the rain and laugh at the embarrassing moments life throws our way. **You get to choose!** The choices may be hard, so choose your hard wisely!

Have you ever just woken up on the wrong side of the bed in the worst mood ever? I challenge you to try this. I hear an eye roll! But don't knock it till you try it! Put on some happy music with a great beat and dance. Seriously! Dance your heart out. Watch your mood shift in just moments. If you are not able to physically dance, still put on that cheerful music and dance in your mind and soul until laughter erupts. Laughter is medicine and brings about great endorphins!

Proverbs 17:22 (ESV) says, "A joyful heart is good medicine, but a crushed spirit dries up the bones."

Let's face it, some people are just jerks! And no matter what we do or don't do they won't like us. I want to challenge you, starting today, to not let someone else's inability to see your value determine your worth. I was asked recently in an interview if I could go back and tell my younger self one thing, what would it be? Honestly, it would be to stop letting other people ruin my day. We are only given one life, it's time to stop giving power and authority to another individual or things ruining the best gift given to us, the present.

I know there are chemical imbalances and physical ailments that affect every area of our lives. Please hear my heart and know this chapter does not come from a place of unrealistic expectations or lack of empathy to where you are. It comes from a place of wanting you not only to *live* your life, but to *enjoy* living the life you've got. I've walked with a handicap, and I continue to. But I have decided to try my hardest to choose joy on the hardest of days and not waste it staying stuck in my funk. And after reading this chapter, I hope you will give it a try too.

Psalm 9:9 NIV reminds us, "The Lord is a refuge for the oppressed, a stronghold in times of trouble."

CHAPTER 11

Broken Vessel

I have had the honor to speak at several Purity Youth Conferences over the years. One analogy I like to use is showing a mosaic picture. When you look at a mosaic, you see tiny little pieces that come together to create a beautiful picture. If you start taking away little pieces throughout the picture, it is going to affect the overall masterpiece. I like to share with the youth that we are each a *unique* and beautiful masterpiece, ultimately created by God, and designed to fulfill His purposes while here on earth. We each have our own race to run and or own plan to accomplish with His guiding hand like a potter molding clay.

The journey we call life is full of different seasons and we all have many pieces that make up the individuals we are. These pieces are intricately woven into our being as the Lord created us in our mother's womb. We were designed for a specific purpose.

Jeremiah 1:5 NIV says, "Before I formed you in the womb I knew you, before you were born, I set you apart; I appointed you as a prophet to the nations."

How do we protect the numerous pieces that make up who we are as a whole? We do this by guarding our hearts, minds, and bodies. We must be careful not to give away pieces of ourselves, realizing the value that each piece has. Giving away pieces can be giving away our bodies to others or showing our bodies to others. Giving away pieces can be giving your heart away to others that won't treasure it. You see, it is always best to save as much of your beautiful mosaic to fulfill your plan and purpose in life; and if you're blessed to marry one day, to share these pieces with your future spouse. When we have given away valuable pieces of ourselves prematurely it leads to heartache and strife in marriage and future relationships.

Time to dig a little deeper...what if your pieces were pilfered from you? What if you were abused and forced to give up parts of yourself and your innocence was stolen? I want you to hear me, dear one. Your mosaic is still beautiful. You are still a unique masterpiece. Why do these terrible things happen in our lives? Because we live in a fallen world with an enemy who seeks to steal, kill and ultimately destroy us (John 10:10). But our God is greater. He doesn't let you slip from the palm of His hand when horrendous situations come. He doesn't abandon you or forget about you. Why does He *allow* horrible things to happen? I don't have the answers to all those questions, and I have found focusing on the *why's and what if's* only makes my heart harden and my mind hard to ease. We may never know the *why*, but God does. He sees the whole picture. Often, we go through difficult things for a purpose. Sometimes it is to heal, to redeem, to grow or to help others through. Sometimes it is to help us learn to forgive.

Have you been able to forgive those who you trusted to protect you and they didn't?

According to rainn.org, looking into sexual abuse cases that were *reported* to law enforcement:

- 93% of juvenile victims knew the perpetrator
- 59% were acquaintances
- 34% were family members
- 7% were strangers to the victim

In fact, eight out of ten rapes are committed by someone known to the victim. Studies have shown more than 50% of victims are abused by someone outside of the family who is very well known and trusted. Evidence that a child has been sexually abused is not always obvious, and many children do not report that they have been abused. My parents asked me numerous times if something had happened to me, I denied it every time. When I started acting out with severe anxiety by pulling out my eyelashes and eyebrows, then eating disorders and emotional instability, they took me to a couple different counselors, and I still denied any sexual abuse. Why? I do not have the answers to this, except to share what I have studied and learned through therapy over the years. When something traumatic happens, it is normal for the brain to suppress the events that occurred and even blackout memories. Also, a child's perception can be altered by the abuser and their memories manipulated. Many times, a child is probably scared of getting in trouble and influenced by the abuser that they did something wrong. I went through extensive therapies including EMDR from a Christian Psychologist to heal from PTSD (Post Traumatic Stress Disorder) in my twenties. After my brain injury, I had numerous memories begin to resurface and I needed a lot of help to navigate such trauma. I believe one of the main reasons I denied the abuse was that denial was my brain's response to childhood trauma which I was unable to process at the time. But God loved me too much to leave me there. He knew the importance of these memories resurfacing so I could face the trauma, forgive, and heal. What you cannot talk about or admit holds power over you and must come to light in order for you to heal.

I'm going to sidebar for a moment to speak to parents. I can't imagine how horrific it is to have one of your children abused in any way, especially sexually. My parents tried all they knew to do to address my behaviors that mirrored abuse. If your child similarly is acting out in numerous ways, don't give up trying to get to their heart and learn what happened. I talked with my parents recently about how lost they felt not knowing what to do further to help me. One thing we discussed that may be helpful to anyone reading this book who is struggling with a similar situation, would be to have a survivor of sexual abuse sit down, and more than once, and develop a safe place with the victim to try and help them come to terms with what has happened to them. The victim must be willing to admit the abuse happened to accept the help they need. It is important to not stop trying to reach your child's wound. You may feel like you're hitting a wall and getting nowhere, but don't give up. Keep asking the Lord for guidance and insight. Seek

Him for creative solutions. Keep nurturing and loving your child, especially through the aggravations, fear, and confusion.

If you are an individual who has been abused, you *must* reach out to a trusted and reliable source to get the help you need. Whether the abuse happened five minutes ago or fifty years ago, it happened. Admit it to yourself and to someone else so you can get on a pathway to properly heal and forgive.

Often, we feel guilty for allowing our thoughts to go to that shameful, dirty place in our past; a deep place where we admit we are angry, upset, and beyond hurt knowing that trusted loved ones didn't keep us safe. We could have been betrayed by a family member, friend, teacher, or even our pastor. Most abuse happens because guards set in place to protect children are let down with someone who should have been trustworthy. Because of that, maybe you are angry with God for allowing it to happen to you. Just know that He does not waste a single trial in our lives, but will use it for His purpose as you find healing and peace. When you bring it to the forefront, He will work it out for your good.

We must also realize the importance of forgiving not only our abusers, but also the ones who should have protected us. Sadly, more often than not, they are one and the same. We cannot control what happens to and around us. The behavior of others is out of our hands. God does allow hard things to impact our lives. We must let go of the blame game and stop looking to hold someone responsible or accountable for what has been done to us. We may never get an acknowledgement of what transpired, and most likely we will never get an apology. But we must forgive anyway. It's for our healing, not theirs.

I'm going to paint a mental picture to help you grasp your beauty in the brokenness. One of my good friends, Erika, gave me a most treasured gift a few years back. It was a beautiful clay vessel that had been broken and then filled with gold in every crack to put the vessel back together. Was the vessel beautiful before? Yes, however, the new vessel was even more uniquely beautiful, being formed and made new in the potter's hand.

Jeremiah 18:5-6 MSG declares, "Then God's message came to me: 'Can't I do just as this potter does, people of Israel?'" God's Decree! "Watch this potter. In the same way that this potter works his clay, I work on you, people of Israel."

I was a broken vessel. I had sharp edges that cut others and continually re-injured myself. I was worn thin, fragile, and tried to put on a tough front. I reacted quickly out of fear and from an offensive perspective. I *over*-shared because I felt my voice was rarely heard and no one understood me, what I was trying to say, or where I was coming from.

Over sharing... let's touch on this for a moment. Have you experienced the awkward moment that you said *too* much, and everyone is side glancing at each other? It is often done because you desire a connection and want to go deeper. But some, actually a LOT, of friendships are surface level. An acquaintance is different than a friendship. Friendship has a deeper emotional magnitude. As I mentioned earlier, I had to learn the brutal way that we usually have a *very* small inner circle. If you take the time to figure that out, you'll do yourself a huge favor and save yourself a world of heartache. Not everyone has your best interest in mind. Not everyone is cheering you on. Not everyone is happy for you. Not everyone wants you to succeed. Take the time to sit in this and weigh out the harsh truths of who *your inner circle* is. You need to be careful who you share your intimate thoughts with. Be careful who you share your failures with. But be even more careful who you share your dreams with. I recently read online in a meme that rings true. "Life is a game of chess. You don't talk, you just play. Don't broadcast your intentions. Act in silence, keep achieving. Why? Because your achievements are your checkmate." Basically, when you succeed and reach your goals it will be known. Let your success speak for itself!

Man, did I struggle with control issues. I was handicap to make a move and scared to not make a move. I would worry about the stupidest little things and literally live in chaos mode worried about the "what if's". After many years of getting nowhere and exhausted from trying to be the CEO of the universe, I learned my *need* to control came from fear. Fear of the unknown. Fear of failing. Fear of pain and heartbreak. Fear of letting others down. Fear of rejection. Fear of losing the ones I loved most in this world. FEAR takes on many different faces. And it is a spirit. Yep, I said that. There are over 360 verses commanding us to "fear not". That is an area you *can* take control over and rebuke when it rears its ugly head in your life. Fear deceives. Have you ever heard the acronym that fear is False Evidence Appearing Real? Your situation may be 100% real, but fear takes it to a whole new level. Do you struggle with control? Dig to find the root of fear, then you'll be able to find freedom.

I also struggled with insecurities and shame because of what had happened to me, and because of being broken, the things I had done in response. I acted out in ways I never thought I would. It's embarrassing to recall. And I lost my ability to say "no". When sexual abuse resurfaced in my life, I became handicapped and let the abuse happen again and again. This occurred many times. As a result, I did many things I am ashamed of to this day. What we need to realize is we *all* have a past. We all have deep dark hidden secrets. We need to bring the darkness to light and admit what we've done, what has happened to us, and repent so we can move on. If we don't deal with our past sins and failures, then they will continually come up in our future lives. Just like weeds in the soil of our hearts. Stop ignoring and shying away from what you have done. What you can't talk about has power over you. It is time to cross the denial bridge to reach victory on the other side.

I felt like a useless cheap vessel that had no value. But the ultimate potter took me in His hands and created a new, stronger, and more intricately beautiful vessel. With my cracks came a purposeful story to share with others. Others might have just skimmed past a vessel perfectly formed and free of cracks, overlooking my story. But *the refining in the fire* worked out my character flaws and helped me shine brighter with His love and light inside of me. Others can now see that I am uniquely set apart. Uniquely beautiful.

When someone hurts us, it leaves a mark. It places a crack in our vessels. If we are not careful to address these cracks, it can shatter our whole vessel. This leads to harder and longer work to repair the damage done. When you are hurt, don't shy away from it, ignoring or burying it. Don't explode onto others, making the cracks worse. Instead, go to the Potter and ask for His help to mold you in His hands and heal your wounds. Invite Him into your broken innermost parts, the hidden shame and deep agony.

Anything and everything can be redeemed with the help of Yahweh, the one true God. We are each broken in some shape or form. He is ready to shine through your brokenness and heal you from the inside out. You my dear one, are a beautiful mosaic masterpiece. And the Lord wants to fill your vessel to overflowing into this broken world. Rick Warren said it beautifully, "In God's garden of grace, even a broken tree can bear fruit. We are all broken."

Psalm 139:13-14 ESV reminds us, "For you formed my inwards parts; you knitted me together in my mother's womb. I praise you, for I am fearfully and wonderfully made."

CHAPTER 12

Brain Game

So much of what ails us goes back to the battles raging in our minds. It's what I refer to as the "brain game." One thing I strive to be is raw and real so I decided to add in this chapter to share some struggles I am currently facing, and how I am determined to win at this *brain game*.

Our brains are truly incredible! The brain has been referred to as "the most complex thing we have yet to discover in the universe." This incredible organ controls our thoughts and actions, keeps things in order, solves problems and executes plans. These executive functions are sometimes called our superpowers. Another amazing thing about our brains is that they are a muscle and can be trained. Did you know there are over one hundred billion nerve cells and contact points in our brains telling us what to do? We rely on our brains for most everything, even breathing!

Honestly, I think *all* of us struggle with the healthy functioning of our brains. Not just those of us who have had a brain injury, developmental issue, or traumatic event happen. Have you ever struggled with depression? How about anxiety? Ever lost sleep over a situation you can't control, then had trouble controlling your emotions? Do you spend hours on a screen, eat foods with preservatives or walk on a planet with pesticides? Do you get *hangry* when you haven't eaten or had your caffeine fix? Hands up every where. Every day we are exposed to things in our daily lives that affect the functioning of our brains. This is serious, and consequently seriously effects the quality of our lives. Thankfully, there is much to be done to help our brains function correctly. Each of us can benefit from learning more about how to detox, and get optimal blood flow into our brains through diet, exercise, supplements and more.

I recently had symptoms rear their ugly head from my brain injury twenty plus years ago. Serious, detrimental symptoms. Symptoms that brought about crippling fear. I did the foolish thing many of us often do, and ignored them for a while hoping it would just go away. Well, said symptoms did *not* go away, and instead, became more frequent and severe.

So off I went for extensive testing and SPECT brain scans *again* to see what was going on neurologically. I told a few family members and close friends that I knew would be prayer warriors and help lift up me up when I had little hope or strength left to push on. And we prayed and prayed. Even with all that praying, the results came back not good. I was heartbroken. I was devastated. And then I was angry! I am supposed to be miraculously healed, so why is this happening?! I literally felt like I was walking through different stages of grief. I even wrestled with feeling like a fool for writing these books and doing the public speaking to encourage others to not give up, when I myself felt like giving up.

But then it hit me, of course I am facing this trial walking through these symptoms. Look at where I have come? Look at the healing and breakthrough I received pouring my heart out through these pages to help others wrestle through their grief, turn to face the storms of life and *grow through* with the help of the one true God who can save us! There was the *why*. And now I had the reason to not give up.

I have found when walking through a trial it is important to learn to master our thoughts in order to gain victory mentally, which ultimately affects us emotionally and physically. We are going to have to face it, and that is what this book is all about. Don't ignore it like I did, get the help. You deserve it!

I am currently walking through a battlefield in my mind and not going through it unscathed. But one thing that has helped me is going back to my gratitude journals to remember the *many* times of breakthrough and healing I've experienced in my life. I also went back through cards and texts from others with encouraging words to soothe my aching heart. Choosing an attitude of gratitude is not easy when walking through hard times, but it is of utmost importance if we want to walk our way to freedom and healing.

I have to get out of my head so often! Y'all, I know it's hard. I am dealing with a prognosis I am heartbroken about. I am having to white knuckle through so much fear. And I am realizing even more the importance of taking those thoughts captive even when we are experiencing every symptom imaginable. Our faith is so much more than our circumstances. Our faith is a muscle, just like our brains, we need to work on growing it daily, even when we don't *feel* like it. Our symptoms do *not* dictate the level of our healing. We have to choose to walk out our faith even when our bodies are not walking in healing. It is not easy, but I have found my greatest weapon to combat these negative and fearful thoughts has been found in my praise. By this, I mean choosing to praise regardless of my pain. I am continuously praising God for my healing, for my wholeness, for His protection and goodness in my life. I know it's not easy. Some days, I can barely lift my head. I feel at times that I am barely surviving moment by moment, but I am here, so God's not done yet. Until God opens a door, praise Him in the hallway!

As we grow and go through trials in life, it is helpful to remember it's not a one and done journey, but God is there to help us handle whatever comes our way. We are reminded of this is John 16:33 "I have told you these things, so that in me you may have peace. In this world you will have trouble. But take heart! I have overcome the world." The amplified version expounds on this by saying to be confident, undaunted, and filled with joy because His conquest is complete, and His victory abiding!

This reassures me that whatever I am facing, He has overcome it already. I tell myself often on those really hard days, "God saw this day!" It's a good reminder to me that He is in whatever I am facing right here, right now. Not only is He right there walking through it with me, but He is not taken by surprise by what I am going through now or will go through in the future.

Be the winner in your brain game and overcome those daunting thoughts with truths found in God's Word. I recently heard a song that said, "If it's not good, then He is not done." I hold tight to this knowing that Yahweh promises in Romans 8:28 are to work all things together for our good. God's got you dear one. He's not done. Keep on keeping on!

CHAPTER 13

Waving the White Flag

This brings me to the latest lesson the Lord has been dealing with me on–surrender.

What does it mean to surrender?

- Cease resistance, submit to authority.
- Give up completely.

How do we know we need to surrender? Think of a situation in your life where you have given it everything you've got, and still, you're nowhere near reaching its full potential. Bottom line–you must relinquish control and give that thing up completely.

That's what surrendering to God is all about. It's about admitting that you can't do everything on your own and that you need help. It's about admitting that there's something bigger than you, something that you can't control.

That *something* is called *life.* And each of our lives

have a purpose. But to achieve that full purpose we must surrender it to the Lord.

What does the Bible say about surrender? Not only are we told in Scripture to surrender our lives to accept the *free gift* of salvation, but also to pursue daily surrender of our sinful, prideful nature. It's ultimately trusting His ways are better than ours.

There is power when we put our trust in God. When you trust in God, you're putting your faith in a power greater than yourself. You're acknowledging that there's something bigger going on in the world and that you need help navigating it. In an essence, your obedience to surrender is your response to God's love for you.

But let's take a moment for some brutal honesty. Have you ever wondered "God, are you there?" This topic is a tricky one. I want to start by clarifying *I know that I know that I know* that God has never left or forsaken me. But what I am talking about the hard seasons when it *feels* like He is nowhere to be found. Or when we *think* he has forgotten us and won't give an answer. I like to refer to these seasons as times of drought.

Going back to our gardens, most of us realize how critical it is to water the soil, seeds, and plants. When there is a drought, the plants do not die immediately. What actually happens is the roots get damaged first. This leads to a secondary effect of weakening the plant making it more susceptible to insects, weeds, pollutants, diseases, and other opportunistic pests. The significance of the drought also affects the plant's production of leaves, seeds, fruit, or flowers. And of course, the ultimate symptom of drought is death.

Let's apply this to our *heart* soil. What constitutes a drought? *Spiritual* drought is when you experience the feeling of abandonment, frustration, fear of the unknown, helplessness and remaining stagnant. It is so important that when these tough seasons of drought come, you choose to remain in obedience. You must surrender every part of your life to Him. He knows what He is doing, even when you don't have a clue! This is the time to dig in with one-on-one time alone with Him and His Word, asking for His guidance and direction.

The Bible promises us that God blesses the one who obediently surrenders to Him.

Proverbs 16:3 NIV instructs us, "Commit to the Lord whatever you do, and he will establish your plans."

Obedience is difficult, especially when things are tough and unclear. But when you surrender to God, you're opening yourself up to His guidance and love. You're permitting Him to work in your life, even when you don't understand what's happening. Surrendering to Him brings clarity and wisdom to your decision-making process. It is letting Him take the lead.

Sometimes, it is tough to follow because we like the *feeling* of leading. It brings a false sense of security in our lives. Sadly, we are often blinded by our desire to have complete control over our lives. We believe we can do it *all* on our *own* and therefore do not trust or rely on God's will or way. Many of us consider surrender a sign of weakness, vulnerability, and defeat. And too often our shame, guilt, and pride prevent us from surrendering completely to God.

Or, how often do we feel that God is moving too slowly, so we sprint ahead and leave Him behind? Oh, I am waving *both* hands in the air for this one! Truth is, there is a purpose for *every* step we take in our lives. His timing is the perfect timing for things to happen. There are lessons to be learned right where we are. Enjoy the world around you. Be present. If God is asking you to wait, be patient. Waiting is not a waste of time when you are waiting on God and His timing. In His perfect timing He will reveal what is next for you.

Oh, the waiting game. It seems so simple to remind others and ourselves to be patient and just hold on and wait. But if you have been waiting for a while, or if you are presently being rushed into a decision that *must* be made, waiting can feel like an eternity. We may need the answers now, so we rush ahead. But sadly, rushed decisions and actions are rarely right, so it is crucial to wait when we are not sure about a situation or a decision. When in doubt do without. Wait for His peace to proceed.

How do we wait? We must wait with the right attitude. Ouch! I know, I am literally writing this to myself as I am in a continual season of what feels like a waiting game for our ministry. The closer something is to your heart or the bigger impact the situation may have on your life and those around you, the harder the waiting game is. Let me encourage you (cough... and myself), God has you exactly where He wants you right here right now. Even when it is not fair, even when it doesn't make sense, even when it leaves you feeling bewildered. You are in this season of waiting for a reason. I am learning in this process that waiting is not only for our growth, but also for our protection.

A beautiful thing happens when you step away from doing what *you* feel is right for yourself and take a step in trusting Him *fully* with your whole life.

Proverbs 3:5-6 NIV, tells us, "Trust in the Lord with all your heart. And do not lean on your own understanding. In all your ways submit to Him, and He will make your paths straight." I have read several devotions on surrender that narrow it down to some basics I like to apply in my own life:

- Submitting to Him is a powerful choice.
- Submitting to Him is a way of letting go of control and fear.
- Submitting to Him is a way of letting go of the *past*, so you can move forward into your *future*.

By surrendering, you are choosing to not fight to control your circumstances and emotions anymore, knowing ultimately you will never win that fight! But rather you can choose to be open and receive whatever comes your way—for better or worse. You are choosing to walk by faith not sight. Martin Luther King Jr said, "Faith is taking the first step, even when you don't see the whole staircase." Oh, I just love that! Even though you might not be able to see where you are going in your life, just keep going! One step at a time. We live under freedom and protection from God's grace.

I recently read an online devotion from Bible.org that shared a tough example of how God took Abraham to the place He seeks to bring each of us. For Abraham, it was a place of total surrender because God was asking him to sacrifice his son. Likewise, God's goal is to bring each of us to that point of ultimate surrender to Him. It sounds scary; but two things ease our fear:

1. Ultimate surrender involves a process. God doesn't just drop or leave us; He is working out something within our character. Refining us in the fire as it says in Proverbs 17:3.
2. When God asks us to surrender, it stems from love. His ways are *always* better than our own, no matter how much we think we have it all together. We are a work in progress; we are never done growing.

James 4:10 says, "Humble yourselves before the Lord, and He will lift you up." Surrendering spiritually means we give up *our plans*, trusting God to have His way in all aspects of our lives, and allowing Him to direct our steps and decisions. This is a learning process. Consider those tough situations where you are dealing with self-soothing habits or addictions and invite God right into the mess while you are literally *in the mess*. We often feel we have to get it all together to come to God, but He wants to meet us right where we are at.

Proverbs 3:5–6 ESV contains one of the best Bible verses for clearly describing the main idea of surrendering to God. It says, "With all your heart, trust in the Lord. And don't rely on your understanding. In all your ways acknowledge Him, and He will make your paths straight."

God asks us to surrender our lives to be "instruments of His righteousness."

Galatians 2 tells us, "Walking with Christ entails constant surrender. And when we surrender, we accept the Holy Spirit to live within us. You will live in faith, knowing that the One to whom we have submitted can make our lives better and will not disappoint us."

Ultimately, when you obey and surrender, your faith will strengthen, and you will find rest and peace in your minds, hearts, and souls. Dissatisfaction, discouragement, and doubt will fade away. You will grow closer to God, and with that closeness comes the courage to face even the most difficult situations. God will protect and sustain you in ways you cannot fathom!

So, it's time. Time to let go of *your* plans and allow God to guide you. God loves you and has had a plan for your life since the beginning; no step along the way has been overlooked. Trust Him and offer up your plans as a sacrifice to your Savior.

Psalm 27:14 ESV encourages us, "Wait for the Lord; be strong, and let your heart take courage; wait for the Lord!"

I think back to when my marriage was hanging by a thread, and I had to fully surrender it *and* Clif to the Lord. When I did, He moved in mighty ways! God moved because I moved out of His way.

The thing about surrendering to God is that we must *continue* choosing it.

Although it is difficult to surrender our will and our ways to God, the impact of our decision to trust God will be felt for generations to come.

I will end my book with a poem I recently wrote on the surrender I am experiencing in my life right now.

I share this to encourage you and remind you that none of us are ever through growing! We will always have new challenges to navigate on the journey of life, but I hope you have found some helpful tactics to apply along the way. More than anything I hope you feel *lighter*! That you have unpacked some of those burdens you've been carrying around. I hope you feel like you can stretch more and relax more now that you have

STUCK IN THE STORM

done the hard work of digging out those stones and stubborn roots in the soil of your heart, and now have the tools to navigate any storms that come your way.

So many goals, aspirations, and dreams
If I'm not trying, I'm failing it seems.
So, I sit back, and examine the picture at hand.
This world tells me to do more–give in to their demands

But the God I know is quiet when chaos abounds.
He tells me *come closer–there's peace to be found.*
But first you must lay down the lists you've created.
Evaluate your schedule–you've become inundated.

How did this happen? I ask in confusion.
Because you sought your own strength, to be your solution.
How do I remedy this problem I have caused?
Simply hand them to Me, they will each be solved.

Fulfilling your purpose–is not completely up to you.
It requires obedience and surrender in all you do.
But what if I'm not doing enough?
Giving Me your all is not giving up.

It's trusting each step of your path to My plan.
I see the whole picture, and I'm here to take your hand.

*So, hand your dreams over to me and don't delay,
I've placed them into your heart, trust me—I know
the way.*

"Maybe you didn't prep and till the soil quite perfectly. Maybe the sun beat down a little too hard. Maybe the rain came too much or not enough by your standards. But is the seed still valuable? Is the seed still powerful enough to produce? The answer is YES. The conditions can vary, but the seed was always the point. Don't stop Sowing." –Nicole Buck

Matthew 9:37AMP informs us, "Then He said to His disciples, 'The harvest is [indeed] plentiful, but the workers are few. So, pray to the Lord of the harvest to send out workers into His harvest.'"

Now is the time. Now is *your* time. Break free and truly live your life.

The End

Appendix

Let's go deeper...

I wanted to dedicate time to diving *deeper* into certain topics covered in the book. The desire is to bring different definitions and insights to the table to digest. Take time to chew on the information given and mediate on the scriptures provided. I hope they shed light and offer counsel and comfort into certain areas of your life you're seeking growth and answers.

Surrender:

- Agreeing to stop fighting, hiding, or resisting.
- Becoming a believer who completely gives up his own will and subjects his thoughts, ideas, and deeds to the will of God.
- Taking a humble position and embracing leadership over you.
- Not giving up on God or on ourselves; but trusting Him, even when do not understand what is happening.
- Giving up your egotistical desires, tapping into your intuition, and allowing yourself to be guided.

- Having absolute faith to realize and accept that God knows the best path for us, even when it seems illogical.
- Becoming more comfortable with "not knowing," and fervently praying for God's strength during the times of uncertainty.
- Striving to be patient and letting God's plan for you unfold naturally and gracefully.
- Knowing the Hebrew translation of "Rapha" means to let go and release.

Letting Go Of Control In Surrendering:

- Contentment in the seasons of waiting.
- Worshipping while waiting.
- Being used as a vessel in the seasons of waiting.
- Trusting blindly.
- Cultivating an attitude of gratitude.
- Not falling into condemnation.
- Choosing healthy new patterns.
- Rejecting old self destructive/self-soothing patterns.
- Embracing the relief of weight lifted off you.
- Seeking peace to calm inner chaos.
- Renewing the mind daily.

- Forgiveness to others and self.
- Releasing criticism and negativity.
- Casting out anxiety (spirit of fear).
- Not understanding and accepting it.
- Not knowing and accepting it.
- Rebuking thoughts of abandonment.
- Uprooting addictions.
- Tearing down strongholds.
- Cessation
- Obedience (not delayed, and continual).
- Learning and growing.
- Blooming through adversity.

Verses To Ponder:

JOB 11:13-19 CEV:

"Surrender your heart to God, turn to Him in prayer, and give up on your sins- even those you do in secret. Then you won't be ashamed; you will be confident and fearless. Your troubles will go away like water beneath a bridge, and your darkest night will be brighter than noon. You will rest safe and secure, filled with hope and emptied of worry. You will sleep without fear and be greatly respected."

APPENDIX

JAMES 4:7 NIV:

"Submit yourselves then to God. Resist the Devil, and he will flee from you."

JAMES 4:10 NIV:

"Humble yourselves before the Lord, and He will lift you up."

JEREMIAH 10:23 NIV

"Lord, I know that people's lives are not their own; it is not for them to direct their steps."

MATTHEW 6:33 NLT:

"Seek the Kingdom of God above all else, and live righteously, and He will give you everything you need."

PROVERBS 23:26 CJB:

"My son, give me your heart; let your eyes observe my ways."

PSALM 9:10 CEBA:

"Those who know your name trust you because you have not abandoned any who seek you, Lord."

ROMANS 12:2 CEB:

"Don't be conformed to the patterns of the world, but be transformed by the renewing of your minds so that you can figure out what God's will is, what is good and pleasing and mature."

1 PETER 5:6-10 CJB:

"Therefore, humble yourselves under the mighty hand of God, so that at the right time He may lift you up. Throw all your anxieties upon Him, because He cares about you. Stay sober, stay alert! Your enemy, the adversary, stalks about like a roaring lion looking for someone to devour. Stand against him, firm in your trust, knowing that your brothers throughout the world are going through the same kinds of suffering. You will have to suffer only a little while; after that, God, who is full of grace, the one who called you to His eternal glory in union with the Messiah, will Himself restore, establish and strengthen you and make you firm."

PHILIPPIANS 2:5-8 NRS:

"Let the same mind be in you that was in Christ Jesus, who though He was in the form of God, did not regard equality with God as something to be exploited, but emptied Himself, taking the form of a slave, being born in human likeness. And being found in human form, He humbled Himself and became obedient to the point of death- even death on a cross."

APPENDIX

PSALM 96:7 TPT:

"Surrender to the Lord YAHWEH,
all you nations and peoples.
Surrender to Him all your pride and strength."

Sin:

1. Hebrew translation: Khata—to fail, to miss the goal.
2. Greek translation: Hamartia—to miss the mark.
3. Transgression of the law of God.
4. Any deliberate action, attitude, or thought that goes against God.

Detriments Of Sin:

- Pain.
- Regret.
- Unknown consequence and repercussions.
- Broken relationships and families.
- Loss of job(s).
- Ruined friendships
- Loss of trust.
- Broken covenants.
- Addictions.
- Death.
- Destruction.

- Turmoil.
- Paranoia.
- Habitual lying.
- Hardened heart and conscious.
- Blind and deafness spiritually.
- Confusion.
- Conflict.
- Chaos.
- Regret.
- Selfishness.
- Pride.
- Lack of empathy.
- Loss of protection/covering.
- Desensitization.
- Dissatisfaction.
- Lack of contentment.

Verses To Ponder:

ROMANS 3:23 NIV:

"For all have sinned and fall short of the glory of God."

1 JOHN 1:8 CEV:

"If we say we have not sinned, we are fooling ourselves, and the truth isn't in our hearts."

APPENDIX

JAMES 4:17 CEV:

"If you do not do what you know is right,
you have sinned."

ROMANS 6:23 NIV:

"For the wages of sin is death, but the gift of God
is eternal life in Christ Jesus our Lord."

GALATIANS 5:19-21 NIV:

"The acts of the flesh are obvious:
sexual immorality, impurity, and debauchery;
idolatry and witchcraft; hatred, discord,
jealousy, fits of rage, selfish ambition,
dissensions, factions, and envy; drunkenness,
orgies, and the like. I warn you, as I did before,
that those who live like this will not inherent
the kingdom of God."

PROVERBS 14:21 NIV:

"Whoever despises their neighbor sins,
but blessed in the one who is kind to the needy."

EPHESIANS 4:26-27 NIV:

"In your anger do not sin.
Do not let the sun go down while you are still angry,
and do not give the devil a foothold."

1 CORINTHIANS 10:13 NIV:

"No temptation has overtaken you except what is common to mankind. And God is faithful; He will not let you be tempted beyond what you can bear. But when you are tempted, He will also provide a way out so you can endure it."

COLOSSIANS 3:5-6 NIV:

"Put to death, therefore, whatever belongs to your earthly nature: sexual immorality, impurity, lust, evil desires and greed, which is idolatry."

ISAIAH 59:2 CEV:

"Your sins are the roadblock between you and your God. That's why He doesn't answer your prayers or let you see His face."

GALATIANS 6:7-8 NIV:

"Do not be deceived; God cannot be mocked. A man reaps what he sows. The one who sows to please his sinful nature, from that nature will reap destruction."

NUMBERS 32:23B NIV:

"You can be sure that your sin will find you out."

APPENDIX

HEBREWS 4:13 NIV:

"Nothing in all creation is hidden from God's sight. Everything is uncovered and laid bare before the eyes of Him who must give account."

Lying:

1. Telling or containing lies, being deliberately untruthful, deceitful, and false.
2. To make an untrue statement with intent to deceive.
3. To create a false misleading impression.
4. Treachery either by words or action.
5. Exaggerated truths.
6. The translation in Hebrew *Sheker*—that which makes you cold.

Consequences Of Lying:

- God absolutely detests lying. It's the act of lying He hates because it is contrary to His truths.
- Lying if often associated with deceit and falsehood which are traits of our old self. We are to die to self and take on the new person hood.

EPHESIANS 4:22-24 NIV:

"You were taught, with regard to your former way of life, to put off your old self, which is being corrupted by deceitful desires; to be made new in the attitude of your minds; and to put on the new self, created to be like God in true righteousness and holiness."

- Lying often leads to other sins such as stealing, cheating, anger, etc...
- It was an act of deception that led to the fall of all of humanity in the Garden of Eden.
- When we lie, we go against God's plan for our lives.
- Lying breaks a commandment from God.
- Lying *always* causes harm to self and others.
- Lying leads to more and more lying which can become a difficult habit to break.
- Once you break someone's trust it is hard to gain back.
- There are always consequences that come from deceitfulness.
- Lying strongly affects our character.
- Lying is considered a sin *against* others and God.
- Lying leads to condemnation.
- Lying leads to spiritual death (and sometimes physical).

- Lying can leave lasting wounds in one's life and relationships.
- Lying separates us from God and being in tune to hearing the Holy Spirit.
- The Bible tells us liars do not enter the kingdom of heaven (Revelation 21:8); this is referred to as the second death—lying without repentance and forgiveness.
- Lying causes stress and strain on our health and can lead to doubt and ability to make wise decisions, and damages our ability to make informed choices.
- Dishonesty has been scientifically proven to put the brain in a heightened state of alert, higher blood pressure, increased heart rate, vasoconstriction, and elevated stress hormones in the blood (Psychology Today).

Verses To Ponder:

EXODUS 20:16 AMP:

"You shall not testify falsely
[that is, lie, withhold, or manipulate the truth]
against your neighbor (any person)."

COLOSSIANS 3:9-10 NIV:

"Do not lie to each other, since you have taken off your old self with its practices and have put on the new self, which is being renewed in knowledge in the image of its Creator."

DEUTERONOMY 18:20 MSG:

"But any prophet who fakes it, who claims to speak in my name something I haven't commanded him to say, or speaks in the name of other gods, that prophet must die."

PROVERBS 6:16-19 NIV:

"There are six things the Lord hates, seven that are detestable to Him: haughty eyes, a lying tongue, hands that shed innocent blood, a heart that devises wicked schemes, feet that are quick to rush into evil, a false witness who pours out lies and a person who stirs up conflict in the community."

JOHN 8:44 NIV:

"You belong to your father, the devil, and you want to carry out your father's desires. He was a murderer from the beginning, not holding to the truth, for there is no truth in him. When he lies, he speaks his native language, for he is a liar and the father of lies."

APPENDIX

LEVITICUS 19:11 NIV:

"Do not steal. Do not lie. Do not deceive one another."

PROVERBS 12:19 NIV:

"Truthful lips endure forever,
but a lying tongue only last a moment."

EPHESIANS 4:25 NIV:

"Therefore, each of you must put off falsehood
and speak truthfully to your neighbor,
for we are all members of one body."

JOHN 14:6 NIV:

"I am the way and the truth and the life.
No one comes to the Father except through Me."

PROVERBS 12:22 NIV:

"The Lord detests lying lips,
but He delights in people who are trustworthy."

PROVERBS 19:5 NIV:

"A false witness will not go unpunished,
and whoever pours out lies will not go free."

PROVERBS 19:9 AMP:

"A false witness will not go unpunished,
and he who breathes lies will perish."

TITUS 1:4 MSG:

"My aim is to raise hopes by pointing the way to life God promised long ago—and He doesn't break promises (God does not lie)."

MATTHEW 5:36-37 MSG:

"In making your speech sound more religious, it becomes less true. Just say 'yes' and 'no.' When you manipulate words to get your own way, you go wrong."

PSALM 51:6 AMP:

"Behold, you desire truth in the innermost being, and in the hidden part [of my heart] you will make me know wisdom."

PROVERBS 13:5 AMP:

"A righteous man hates lies, but a wicked man is loathsome, and he acts shamefully."

PROVERBS 14:5 NIV:

"An honest witness does not deceive, but a false witness pours out lies."

ZEPHANIAH 3:13 AMP:

"The remnant of Israel will do no wrong nor speak lies, nor will a deceitful tongue be found in their mouths;

APPENDIX

for they will eat and lie down with no one to make them tremble and feel afraid."

DEUTERONOMY 5:20 CSB:

"Do not give dishonest testimony against your neighbor."

PSALM 34:12-13 NLT:

"Does anyone want to live a life that is long and prosperous? Then keep your tongue from speaking evil and your lips from telling lies!"

PROVERBS 19:5 NIV:

"A false witness will not go unpunished, and a liar will be destroyed."

REVELATION 22:14-15 ESV:

"Blessed are those who wash their robes, so that they may have the right to the tree of life and that they may enter the city by the gates. Outside are the dogs and sorcerers and the sexually immoral and murderers and idolaters, and everyone who loves and practices falsehood."

1 JOHN 3:18 NLT:

"Dear children, let's not merely say that we love each other, let us show the truth by our actions."

PSALM 51:6 ESV:

"Behold you [God] delight in truth
in the inward being, and you teach me wisdom
in the secret heart."

PSALM 58:3 ESV:

"The wicked are estranged from the womb;
they go astray from birth, speaking lies."

PSALM 101:7 NLT:

"I will not allow deceivers to serve in my house,
and liars will not stay in my presence."

JEREMIAH 17:9-10 ESV:

"The heart is deceitful above all things,
and desperately sick; who can understand it?
I the LORD search the heart and test the mind,
to give every man according to his ways,
according to the fruit of his deeds."

PSALM 5:4-6 GW:

"You are not a God who takes pleasure in
wickedness. Evil will never be your guest.
Those who brag cannot stand in your sight.
You hate troublemakers, you destroy those who
tell lies. The LORD is disgusted with
bloodthirsty and deceitful people."

APPENDIX

ROMANS 3:4B NLT:

"Even if everyone else is a liar, God is true.
As the scriptures say about him,
'You will be proved right in what you say,
and you will win your case in court.'"

1 TIMOTHY 4:1-2 NIV:

"The Spirit clearly says that in later times some will abandon the faith and follow deceiving spirits and things taught by demons. Such teachings come through hypocritical liars, whose consciences have been seared as with a hot iron."

PROVERBS 12:19 NLT:

"Truthful words stand the test of time
but lies are soon exposed."

JOHN 4:24 NIV:

"God is spirit, and His worshipers must worship in the spirit and in truth."

Faith:

1. Complete trust or confidence in someone or something.
2. Strong belief in God or in the doctrines of religion.

3. Trusting in God and His Word based on evidence without total proof.
4. An allegiance to duty or a person (loyalty).
5. Fidelity to one's promises, sincerity of intentions.
6. Something believed with strong conviction.
7. Belief without question.
8. In Hebrew "Emunah" a life full of reliance upon Yahweh.

Living A Life In Faith:

- Learning to walk through something not knowing what the outcome will be.
- Blindly trusting that God works all things for our good *IF* we love Him and are *called* according to His purpose (Romans 8:28).
- Seeing is *not* believing. Childlike faith is what we are called to (Matthew 18:3).
- Asking Yahweh to reveal Himself to you and your children, ask specifically for a divine encounter.
- Securing our faith happens when we grow in our relationship with Him by spending time in His Word and prayer.
- Walking by faith is seeing our circumstances and others from a heavenly perspective instead of a worldly one.

- Taking on maturity to realize what is seen is temporary, but what is unseen is eternal.
- Having an eternal perspective so we can feel His presence and guidance in the here and now.
- Living our lives according to God's commands and promises.
- Walking by faith and not sight means even though you might not be able to see where you are going, just keep moving, don't allow yourself to get stuck in fear of the "what ifs".
- Trusting that God sees the *whole* picture and relying on Him as our guide.
- Walking by faith is rejoicing and having a heart of gratitude during the hardest of times knowing God is still on the throne and in control.
- Walking by faith is living our lives in light of an eternal mindset and consequences.
- Walking by faith is fearing God more than man; obeying His commands even when it conflicts with man's commands; choosing righteousness over sin, no matter the cost; trusting God in every circumstance; and believing God rewards those who seek Him (Got Questions Ministries).

Verses to Ponder:

2 CORINTHIANS 4:18 NIV:

"For we fix our eyes not on what is seen, but on what is unseen, since what is seen is temporary, but what is unseen is eternal."

2 CORINTHIANS 5:16 AMP:

"So, from now on we regard no one from a human point of view [according to worldly standards and values]. Though we have known Christ from a human point of view, now we no longer know Him in this way."

HEBREWS 11:1 ASV:

"Now faith is the assurance of things hoped for, the conviction of the things not seen."

Hebrews 11:6 NIV:

"And without faith it is impossible to please God, because anyone who comes to Him must believe that He exists and that He rewards those who earnestly seek Him."

PROVERBS 3:5-6 MSG:

"Trust God from the bottom of your heart; don't try to figure out everything you do,

everywhere you go;
He's the one who will keep you on track."

MARK 9:23 NIV:

"Everything is possible for the one who believes."

EPHESIANS 2:8-10 NIV:

"For it is by grace you have been saved,
through faith-and this is not from yourselves,
it is the gift of God-not by works,
so that no one can boast.
For we are God's handiwork,
created in Christ Jesus to do good works,
which God prepared in advance for us to do."

MATTHEW 17:20B ESV:

"For truly, I say to you, if you have faith like a grain
of mustard seed, you will say to this mountain,
move from here to there, and it will move,
and nothing will be impossible for you."

MATTHEW 21:22 ESV:

"And whatever you ask in prayer,
you will receive, if you have faith."

2 CORINTHIANS 5:7 ESV:

"For we walk by faith, not by sight."

JAMES 1:6 NIV:

"But when you ask, you must believe and not doubt, because the one who doubts is like a wave of the sea, blown and tossed by the wind."

JAMES 1:3 ESV:

"For you know that the testing of your faith produces steadfastness."

1 JOHN 5:4 ESV:

"For everyone who has been born of God overcomes the world. And this is the victory that has overcome the world–our faith."

1 TIMOTHY 6:11-12A ESV:

But as for you, O man of God, flee these things. Pursue righteousness, godliness, faith, love, steadfastness, gentleness. Fight the good fight of faith.

ROMANS 1:17 AMP:

"For in the gospel the righteousness of God is revealed, both springing from faith and leading to faith [disclosed in a way that awakens more faith]. As it is written and forever remains written, the just and upright shall live by faith."

APPENDIX

JOHN 7:38 AMP:

"He who believes in me [who adheres to, trusts in, and relies on me], as the scripture has said, from his innermost being will flow continually rivers of living water."

ROMANS 10:11 NIV:

"As scripture says, anyone who believes in Him will never be put to shame."

JOHN 20:29 AMP:

"Jesus said to him, 'Because you have seen me, do you now believe? Blessed [happy, spiritually secure, and favored by God] are they who did not see [me] and yet believed [in me].'"

ROMANS 10:17 ESV:

"So faith comes from hearing, and hearing through the Word of Christ."

MATTHEW 6:33 ESV:

"But seek first the kingdom of God and His righteousness, and all these things will be added to you."

Hearing from God:

1. The process, function, or power of perceiving.
2. Sense of peace or joy that covers your entire being in a moment of chaos.
3. Communication through prayer, scriptures, sermons, and communities of believers.
4. Hearing from the Lord in circumstances such as dreams, feelings, and even nature.
5. Hearing from and understanding what Yahweh is saying is critical for our spiritual growth and maturity.
6. Translation in Hebrew "Shema" means to which a believer receives the word.

How We Can Hear from God:

- Sometimes it's attaining wisdom in a situation requiring intuition.
- Applying the principles learned in the Word to our daily lives.
- Living a life free of sin and softening the heart and consciousness to hear clearly the promptings of the Holy Spirit.
- Walk with God, be close to Him, in communication with Him throughout the day.

- Serve in areas God calls you to. We are all called to serve.
- Silence everything and everyone around you and sit and listen.
- Do not delay in obedience; delayed obedience is disobedience.
- Fast and pray.
- Read AND study the Word of God.
- Do not be of the world taking part in activities contrary to the Word.
- Ask Him to specifically reveal himself to you and minister to you.
- Be open to receive from Him.
- Be humble and teachable.
- Take time to enjoy His creation; sit in it, marvel at it, let God reveal himself to you in the blessings found in nature.
- Take time for silent meditation. Silence and prayer are *not* the same thing. Prayer is a two-way conversation, where silence takes discipline and teaches us to listen.
- Ask for *specific* wisdom and understanding in areas needed.
- Look for kisses from heaven. These are unexpected blessings throughout the day that are reminders He is close by.

- Journal after time in prayer or during difficult times. Sit in silence, turn off your phone and ask Him to speak. Then write down whatever comes to mind. It may be a picture, number, color, or verse, etc. Jot down what pours out of your heart.
- Cultivate an attitude of gratitude. When we are closed off and bitter we do not hear or see clearly.
- Seek *Godly* counsel from a *trusted* source.
- Reach out to prayer warriors who will have your back in battle.
- It takes time to know someone. How much time are you investing into your relationship with Christ?
- Take bites of the *bread of life* (the Word) throughout the day. Put verses around your home or car, and on your screensavers. Just like you need food to sustain your physical life, you need spiritual food to sustain your spiritual life.
- What you put in comes out. Be careful what you're filling your mind, heart, and time with. It can hinder you hearing clearly from the Lord or hearing from Him at all.

- Have the maturity to realize when He feels silent, He has not abandoned you. A lot of times it is because He is working out something in our hearts and character, or it may be for our protection
- Your spiritual maturity is determined by your recovery rate, how quickly to get back you.

Verses to Ponder:

PSALM 78:1 AMP:

"Listen, O my people, to my teaching;
Incline your ears to the words of my mouth
[and be willing to learn]."

ISAIAH 30:21 NIV:

"Whether you turn to the right or to the left,
your eyes will hear a voice behind you, saying,
this is the way; walk in it."

JEREMIAH 33:3 NIV:

"Call to me and I will answer you and tell you great and unsearchable things you do not know."

PSALM 29:3 ESV:

"The voice of the Lord is over the waters; the God of glory thunders, the Lord, over many waters."

JOHN 10:27 AMP:

"The sheep that are my own hear my voice and listen to me; I know them, and they follow me."

ROMANS 10:17 NIV:

"Consequently, faith comes from hearing the message, and the message is heard through the Word about Christ."

ISAIAH 55:3 AMP:

"Incline your ear [to listen] and come to me; hear, so that your soul may live; and I will make an everlasting covenant with you, according to the faithful mercies [promised and] shown to David."

JOHN 8:31-32 AMP:

"So, Jesus was saying to the Jews who had believed him, "if you abide in My Word [continually obeying My teachings and living in accordance with them, then] you are truly My disciples. And you will know the truth [regarding salvation], and the truth will set you free [from the penalty of sin]."

HEBREWS 2:1 AMP:

"For this reason [that is, because of God's final revelation in His Son Jesus and because of Jesus' superiority to the angels] we must pay much closer attention than ever to the things that we have heard, so that we do not [in any way] drift away from truth."

JOHN 6:63 AMP:

"It is the Spirit who gives life; the flesh conveys no benefit [it is of no account]. The words I have spoken to you are spirit and life [providing eternal life]."

JOHN 17:17 AMP:

"Sanctify them in the truth [set them apart for your purposes, make them holy]; your Word is truth."

2 TIMOTHY 3:16 AMP:

"All scripture is God-breathed [given by divine inspiration] and is profitable for instruction, for conviction [of sin], for correction [of error and restoration to obedience], for training in righteousness [learning to live in conformity to God's will, both publicly and privately, behaving honorably with personal integrity and moral courage]."

Redemption:

1. The action of saving or being saved from sin, error or evil.
2. The action of regaining or gaining possession of something in exchange for payment or clearing a debt
3. Atoning for guilt, a fault or mistake made.
4. Being delivered from the consequences of sin.
5. Deliverance, rescuing, reclaiming, and saving.
6. The translation in Hebrew *Ga'al* also means turnover, ransom, and liberation of slaves.

Our Redemption Through Christ:

- Christ worked on our behalf to ransom us at the price of His own life.
- He secured our deliverance from the bondage and condemnation of our sins.
- God's grace covers everything.
- We live under freedom found in God's grace.
- The only thing that healed and covered everything—the great divide between God and man—was Christ's blood and resurrection.
- The Holy Spirit is what transforms our hearts.
- Work in His grace not in your own efforts.

- His redemption is freely available to us.
- Repentance is *not* the same as salvation.
- God defeated the enemy and death and set His children free through the redemption of His one and only Son laying His life down for us.
- Through Jesus' death and resurrection our redemption is secured for all who believe in Him and accept Him as their Lord and Savior.
- Christ won back eternal life conquering death.
- He secured our deliverance from the bondage and all condemnation of our sins.
- Jesus reminds us grace is how we move as His followers, and there is immeasurable value in *all* acts of kindness.

Verses to Ponder:

EPHESIANS 1:7 NIV

"In Him we have redemption through His blood, the forgiveness of sins, in accordance with the riches of God's grace."

GALATIANS 1:4 MSG:

"We know the meaning of those words because Jesus Christ rescued us from this evil world, where in by offering Himself as a sacrifice for our sins. God's plan is that we all experience that rescue."

GALATIANS 2:20 ESV:

"I have been crucified with Christ. It is no longer I who live, but Christ who lives in me. And the life I now live in the flesh I live by faith in the Son of God, who loved me and gave Himself for me."

GALATIANS 3:13 ESV:

"Christ redeemed us from the curse of the law by becoming a curse for us for it is written, cursed is everyone who is hanged on a tree."

HEBREWS 9:15 ESV:

"Therefore, He is the mediator of a new covenant, so that those who are called may receive the promised eternal inheritance, since a death has occurred that redeems them from the transgressions committed under the first covenant."

ISAIAH 44:22 ESV:

"I have blotted out your transgressions like a cloud and your sins like mist; return to me, for I have redeemed you."

APPENDIX

2 PETER 3:9 NAS:

"The Lord is not slow about His promise,
as some count slowness, but is patient toward you,
not wishing for any to perish but for all
to come to repentance."

ACTS 3:19 MSG:

"Now it's time to change your ways!
Turn to face God so He can wipe away your sins,
and pour out showers of blessing to refresh you."

JOHN 3:16 ESV:

"For God so loved the world,
that He gave His only son, that whoever believes
in Him should not perish but have eternal life."

JOHN 10:10 ESV:

"The thief comes only to steal and kill
and destroy. I came that they may have life
and have it more abundantly."

PSALM 107:2 ESV:

"Let the redeemed of the Lord say so,
whom He has redeemed from trouble."

ROMANS 5:10 NIV:

"For if, while we were God's enemies, we were
reconciled to Him through the death of His Son,

how much more, having been reconciled,
shall we be saved through His life!"

1 CORINTHIANS 1:30 NAS:

"But by His doing you are in Christ Jesus,
who became to us wisdom from God, and
righteousness and sanctification, and redemption."

1 PETER 1:18-19 NIV:

"For you know that it was not with perishable
things such as silver or gold that you were
redeemed from the empty way of life handed down
to you from your ancestors, but with the precious
blood of Christ, a lamb without blemish or defect."

ROMANS 10:9-10 NIV:

"If you declare with your mouth Jesus is Lord
and believe in your heart that God raised Him
from the Dead, you will be saved. For if with
your heart that you believe and are justified,
and it is with your mouth that you profess your
faith and are saved."

LAMENTATIONS 3:57-58 NIV:

"You came near when I called you, and you said
do not fear. You, Lord, took up my case;
you redeemed my life."

APPENDIX

COLOSSIANS 1:12-14 NIV:

"And giving joyful thanks to the Father, who has qualified you to share in the inheritance of His holy people in the kingdom of light. For He has rescued us from the dominion of darkness and brought us into the kingdom of the Son He loves, in whom we have redemption, the forgiveness of sins."

COLOSSIANS 1:20-22 NIV:

"And through Him to reconcile to Himself all things, whether things on earth or things in heaven, buy making peace through His blood, shed on the cross. Once you were alienated from God and were enemies in your minds because of your evil behavior. But now He has reconciled you by Christ's physical body through death to present you holy in His sight, without blemish and free from accusation."

PSALM 130:7 ESV:

"O Israel, Hope in the Lord! For with the Lord there is steadfast love, and with Him is plentiful redemption."

TITUS 2:14 ESV:

"Who gave Himself for us to redeem us from all lawlessness and to purify for Himself a people for

His own possession who are zealous
for good works."

PSALM 111:9 ESV:

"He sent redemption to His people;
He has commanded His covenant forever.
Holy and awesome is His name!"

1 CORINTHIANS 6:20 ESV:

"For you were bought with a price.
So, therefore glorify God with your body."

MATTHEW 20:28 ESV:

"Even as the Son of Man came not to be served but to serve and give His life as a ransom for many."

ROMANS 3:23-24 ESV:

"For all have sinned and fall short of the glory of God, and are justified by His grace as a gift, through the redemption that is in Christ Jesus."

ROMANS 6:23 ESV:

"For the wages of sin is death, but the free gift of God is eternal life in Christ Jesus our Lord."

PSALMS 34:22 ESV:

"The Lord redeems the life of His servants; none of those who take refuge in Him will be condemned."

APPENDIX

1 KINGS 1:29 ESV:

"And the king swore, saying, 'as the Lord lives, who has redeemed my soul out of every adversity.'"

ACTS 4:12 ESV:

"And there is salvation in no one else, for there is no other name under heaven given among men by which we must be saved."

Fear:

1. Awareness or realization.
2. A natural and, in its purpose, beneficent feeling, arising in the presence or anticipation of danger, and moving to its avoidance.
3. Having a deep respect and honor for God rather than being scared of Him.
4. Helps us survive, protects us when needed, and at times, helps us to learn and focus on what is more important.
5. An unpleasant emotion caused by the belief that someone or something is dangerous, likely to cause pain or a threat.
6. The threat of harm real or imagined.
7. The translation in Hebrew *Yirah* means to fear a known thing.

8. The translation in Hebrew *Yirat Adonia* means the fear of the Lord.

Different Types Of Fear: Unhealthy Fear

- FEAR–False Evidence Appearing Real
- Fear can often distort the reality of the situation.
- Fear can have numerous negative effects on a person's health and well-being, including physical, emotional, mental, spiritual, and environmental consequences (study from the University of Minnesota).
- *Physically*–fear weakens the immune system, increases the risk of cardiovascular disease, and can cause gastrointestinal issues. It can lead to decreased fertility. Fear can lead to accelerated aging and premature death. Fear can also lead to kidney disease and vision problems. Fear is stored in the stomach and intestines. Fear causes endocrine system dysfunction, autonomic nervous system alterations, sleep/wake cycle disruptions, eating disorders, and alterations in the HPA axis (AJMC).
- *Emotionally*–fear can cause dissociation from oneself and others, frequent mood swings, obsessive- compulsive thoughts and behaviors. It can also lead to numerous types of anxiety.

- *Mentally*—fear can impair memory and cause damage to certain parts of the brain. Fear also leads to fatigue, clinical depression, PTSD, and panic attacks. Fear is programmed into the nervous system and works like an instinct. And fear affects the brain's ability to learn and store information.
- *Environmentally*—fear can handicap one from moving on or even changing locations (fear generating situations). Fear can entrap one to not feel safe to leave their home. It prevents them from engaging in activities or socializing (AJMC).
- *Spiritually*—fear can lead to bitterness towards God and others. Confusion and distrust with God or religion. And fear can lead to despair related to perceived loss of spiritually (AJMC).

Healthy Fear—Fear Of God:

- A deep, from-the-heart reverence and awe for the Lord.
- The right view of the holiness of God.
- A blessing of the new covenant with Christ.
- Fear of God drives away fear of people.

- Fear of God leads to joy.
- Respecting and honoring that God is the ultimate authority.
- Reveling in the fact God is sovereign and powerful.
- To fear God is to esteem, respect, honor, venerate and adore Him above anyone or anything else (faithgateway).
- When we fear God, we take on His heart. We love what He loves, and we hate what He hates (faithgateway).

Verses To Ponder On Healthy Fear Of The Lord:

DEUTERONOMY 10:12 NIV:

"And now Israel, what does the Lord your God ask of you but to fear the Lord your God, to walk in obedience to Him, to love Him, to serve the Lord your God with all your heart and with all your soul."

JOB 28:28 NIV:

"And He said to the human race, 'The fear of the Lord-that is wisdom, and to shun evil is understanding.'"

APPENDIX

PSALM 33:8 NIV:

"Let all the earth fear the Lord;
let all the people of the world revere Him."

PSALM 34:9 NIV:

"Fear the Lord, you His holy people,
for those who fear Him lack nothing."

PSALM 86:11 NIV:

"Teach me your way, Lord, that I may rely on your faithfulness; give me an undivided heart, that I may fear your name."

PROVERBS 1:7 NIV:

"The fear of the Lord is the beginning of knowledge, but fools despise wisdom and instruction."

PROVERBS 3:7 NIV:

"Do not be wise in your own eyes;
fear the Lord and shun evil."

PROVERBS 8:13 NIV:

"To fear the Lord is to hate evil;
I hate pride and arrogance,
evil behavior and perverse speech."

PROVERBS 14:26-27 NIV:

"Whoever fears the Lord has a secure fortress,
and for their children it will be a refuge.
The fear of the Lord is a fountain of life,
turning a person from the snares of death."

ECCLESIASTES 12:13 NIV:

"Now all has been heard; here is the conclusion in the matter: Fear God and keep His commandments, for this is the duty of all mankind."

MATTHEW 10:28 NIV:

"Do not be afraid of those who kill the body but cannot kill the soul. Rather, be afraid of the One who can destroy both soul and body in hell."

LUKE 1:50 NIV:

"His mercy extends to those who fear Him, from generation to generation."

PHILIPPIANS 2:12-13 NIV:

"Therefore, my dear friends, as you have always obeyed—not only in my presence, but now much more in my absence—continue to work out your salvation with fear and trembling, for it is God who works in you to will and to act in order to fulfill His good purpose."

APPENDIX

PSALM 19:9 NIV:

"The fear of the Lord is pure, enduring forever.
The decrees of the Lord are firm,
all of them are righteous."

PSALM 112:1 NIV:

"Praise the Lord. Blessed are
those who fear the Lord,
who find great delight in His commands."

PSALM 25:14 NIV:

"The Lord confides in those who fear Him;
He makes His covenant known to them."

PROVERBS 19:23 NIV:

"The fear of the Lord leads to life;
then one rests content, untouched by trouble."

PSALM 111:10 NIV:

"The fear of the Lord is the beginning of wisdom; all who follow His precepts have good understanding. To Him belongs eternal praise."

Verses On Overcoming Unhealthy Fear:

ISAIAH 41:10 NIV:

"So do not fear, for I am with you;
do not be dismayed, for I am your God.

I will strengthen you and help you;
I will uphold you with my righteous right hand."

DEUTERONOMY 31:6 NIV:

"Be strong and courageous. Do not be afraid or terrified because of them, for the Lord your God goes with you; He will never leave you nor forsake you."

PSALM 34:4-5 NIV:

"I sought the Lord, and He answered me
and delivered me from all my fears.
Those who look to Him are radiant,
and their faces are never covered with shame."

PSALM 23:4 ESV:

"Even though I walk through the valley of
the shadow of death, I will fear no evil,
for you are with me, your rod and your staff,
they comfort me."

PSALM 56:3-4 ESV:

"When I am afraid, I put my trust in You.
In God, whose Word I praise- in God I trust.
I will not be afraid. What can man do to me?"

APPENDIX

PSALM 27:1 ESV:

"The Lord is my light and my salvation; whom shall I fear? The Lord is the stronghold of my life; of who shall I be afraid?"

PSALM 46:1-3 ESV:

"God is our refuge and strength, a very present help in trouble. Therefore, we will not fear though the earth gives way, though the mountains be moved into the heart of the sea, though its waters roar and foam, though the mountains tremble at the swelling."

ISAIAH 41:13 ESV:

"For I, the Lord your God, hold your right hand; it is I who say to you 'Fear not, I am the One who helps you.'"

JOHN 14:27(ESV)

"Peace, I leave with you; my peace I give to you. Not as the world gives do I give to you. Let not your hearts be troubles, neither let them be afraid."

PSALM 91:4-5 ESV:

"He will cover you with His pinions, and under His wings and you will find refuge;

His faithfulness is a shield and buckler.
You will not fear the terror of the night,
nor the arrow that flies by day."

GENESIS 50:21 ESV:

"'So do not fear; I will provide for you and your little ones.' Thus, He comforted them and spoke kindly to them."

DEUTERONOMY 3:22 ESV:

"You shall not fear them, for it is the Lord your God who fights for you."

JOSHUA 8:1 ESV:

"And the Lord said to Joshua, 'Do not fear and do not be dismayed. Take all the fighting men with you, and arise, go up to Ai. See, I have given into your hand the king of Ai, and his people, his city, and his land.'"

PSALM 27:3 ESV:

"Though an army encamps against me,
my heart shall not fear; though war arise against me,
yet I will be confident."

PSALM 115:11 ESV:

"You who fear the Lord, trust in the Lord!
He is their help and their shield."

APPENDIX

ISAIAH 35:4 ESV:

"Say to those who have an anxious heart,
'Be strong; fear not! Behold, your God will come
with vengeance, with the recompense of God.
He will come and save you."

JEREMIAH 42:11 ESV:

"Do not fear the king of Babylon,
of whom you are afraid. Do not fear him,
declares the Lord, for I am with you,
to save you and to deliver you from his hand."

ISAIAH 43:1(ESV)

"But now thus says the Lord, He who created you,
O Jacob, He who formed you, O Israel:
'Fear not, for I have redeemed you;
I have called you by name, you are mine.'"

LAMENTATIONS 3:57 ESV:

"You came near when I called on you; you said,
'Do not fear!'"

JOEL 2:21 ESV:

"Fear not, O land; be glad and rejoice,
for the Lord has done great things!"

MATTHEW 10:26 ESV:

"So have no fear of them,
for nothing is covered that will not be revealed,
or hidden that will not be known."

MATTHEW 10:31 ESV:

"Fear not, therefore;
you are of more value than many sparrows."

LUKE 2:10 ESV:

"And the angel said to them,
'Fear not, for behold,
I bring you good news of great joy
that will be for all the people.'"

LUKE 12:32 ESV:

"Fear not, little flock, for it is your Father's good
pleasure to give you the kingdom."

PHILIPPIANS 2:12 ESV:

"Therefore, my beloved, as you have always obeyed,
so now, not only as in my presence but much more
in absence, work out your own salvation with
fear and trembling."

2 TIMOTHY 1:7 ESV:

"For God has not given us a spirit to fear,
but of power and love and self-control."

APPENDIX

HEBREWS 13:6 ESV:

"So, we can confidently say, 'The Lord is my helper; I will not fear; what can man do to me?'"

1 JOHN 4:18 ESV:

"There is no fear in love, but perfect love casts out fear. For fear has to do with punishment, and whoever fears has not been perfected in love."

REVELATION 1:17 ESV:

"When I saw Him, I fell at His feet as though dead. But He laid His right hand on me, saying, 'Fear not, I am the first and the last.'"

www.ingramcontent.com/pod-product-compliance
Lightning Source LLC
Chambersburg PA
CBHW070613170426
43200CB00012B/2677